What others are saying about The Mary Group:

Consciously working together with Mary for the last decade has been a catalyst for growth that astounds me on a daily basis. I could use many terms to describe their role in my life—mentor, teacher, translator, butt-kicker, antagonist, joker. I feel I'll just stick with friend.
   —Don (the awkward Walrus) Murphy, Retired Air Traffic Controller

❦ ❦ ❦

Mary has been the most loving of hands lending just the right amount of support in empowering me to remember who I truly am. They have helped me to look around inside myself and find the wholeness that has always been there but not always known; and assisted in my transformation from a victim who only knew how to survive into a powerful creator that is full of bliss and joy for every moment of her ecstatic life! I am eternally grateful and forever in love with Mary!
   —Tracy Ostrand, Founder of Turn Your Shine On

❦ ❦ ❦

I met the Marys when I was experiencing several difficult transitions in my life. The Marys surrounded me with unconditional love and kindness. They have shared their wisdom and given me the tools to create an expansive, yummy and ecstatic life.
   —Andrea J. Weisbond, Author and Entrepreneur

❦ ❦ ❦

What I have taken in of the wisdom of the Marys, has opened me up to the knowing of myself. My life has been forever changed. It is a path worth traveling.
   —Louis (Skip) Weiss, Publisher, *Chicago Health Magazine*

❦ ❦ ❦

For more than a decade, I have been graced with the experience of regular encounters with the Mary Group. They have touched down into every corner of my life with their gifts of wisdom, insight, acceptance and profound love. What they offer is a way home through all that needs healing to all that is best within us. I am forever grateful.
   —Julia Doggart, PhD, Author of *Return*, Owner of Crafted Essence

❦ ❦ ❦

I knew that I was afraid deep inside, that I felt alone and lost. With Mary, I learned about my innocence, about my truth, and my own unique wisdom and guidance...I am living what it means to be whole and to be free.
                    —Elizabeth Jo, Life Alchemist

MARY is expressing what we have always known and what we have never known before. Truth. Wisdom. Love. Grace. The teachings expand and deepen as we each open to receive the offerings. Moving with the laughter and playful spirit of the Mary Group I feel seen and supported, seeing and supporting my Self. Ah, and Horatio...it's wonderful to have a giant among us!
                    —Lori Lovens, Innovation and Engagement Activist

                          ❧ ❧ ❧

I had spent most of my life trying to understand myself and to know who I am. I had a pretty good idea too, then a few years ago, I began talking with the Marys. Mary has been and continues deepening and extending my understanding and is guiding me to a freeing with and in myself I never knew could exist. Now I know there is more, a delicious more to exchange with.
                    —Steve Hall, Creator of Stress Energetics

                          ❧ ❧ ❧

I have never lived so free, creative, joy-filled and at peace...ever. I am forever grateful to The Mary Group and Jacque and Don Nelson for creating this opening for me.
                    —Kathleen Aharoni, Movement & Life Coach, Author of
 I breathe my own breath! (a children's book inspired by Mary's teachings)

Living Without Edges

Teachings from the Loft View

Other books and offerings from Jacque and Don Nelson:

Morning Messages From Mary:
Illuminating the Path to a Life Without Edges

Please visit www.TheMaryGroup.com
for recordings of meditations and other works
by The Mary Group.

Living Without Edges

Edges

Teachings from the Loft View

The Mary Group

with

Jacque and Donald Nelson

RADIANT HEART PRESS
Milwaukee, Wisconsin

Published with delight by
Radiant Heart Press
An imprint of HenschelHAUS Publishing, Inc.
2625 S. Greeley Street, Suite 201
Milwaukee, WI 53207
www.HenschelHAUSbooks.com

All HenschelHAUS titles, imprints, and distributed lines
are available at special quantity discounts for educational,
institutional, fund-raising, or sales promotion.

ISBN: 978-1-59598-128-8
E-ISBN: 978159598-293-3
LCCN: 2013956016

Library of Congress Cataloging-in-Publication
data available on request.

Cover and author photographs by Donald Nelson.

Printed in the United States of America.

*This book is dedicated to our now-grown children,
Michelle and Dustin Eckhardt.*

*We are grateful to them for their willingness to grow up
in a perhaps unusual household with
a variety of amazing people and gatherings.*

*We are so very proud of who you have each become
as the powerful and continuous Creators
of your own beautiful lives.
It is, and always will be, our honor to breathe, love,
and discover side by side with you both.*

Table of Contents

Acknowledgments

We would like to thank our treasured friends of "The Tuesday Night Group," who, for over nine years, in one combination or another, came to our home and met weekly with us and Mary. The diversity of this group and their willingness to delve into themselves and hold honoring space for one another allowed Mary close-up and personal access to and exploration of the intricate human experience. The ongoing weekly commitment of this group to come together in circle and dive—sometimes tenaciously and other times tenderly—into the intimate spaces within and pull their true selves out, through Mary's guidance and insight, was and remains soul-opening. This gave Mary a diverse experience with the ways in which humans move, receive, allow, shift, grow, reject, ebb, and flow. This inspired the way and the richness of content and delivery that Mary now provides to the thousands of people who have and continue to come through our lives.

Don and I thank each of you from the most expansive places in our hearts for letting us "cut our teeth" with you and Mary. It was a very significant adventure and one we enjoyed, appreciated and grew from immensely through the years. We love and believe in you—Deb, Claudette, Doug, Jeanette, John, Judy, Sandra, Julia, and Daniel—and thank you beyond the vibration that words can hold for your believing in us and yourselves and for challenging and loving Mary for all these years.

We would also like to express our ongoing infinite gratitude to all of our amazing friends who have moved with us, and continue to do so, in a variety of currently ongoing Mastery Circles. This allows us to take our work with Mary into a whole new exploration and revealing of soul-expanding truths that open each of us and the world to living in Union. Thank you!

How It All Began ...

the Marys and the wisdoms they teach have been weaving their way into every aspect of our lives since March of 2000.

Prior to that time, my husband Don and I had been living pretty mainstream lives; Don had worked in the printing industry for twenty years and I was a human resource director for a mid-sized nonprofit organization. While we both knew we wanted to step "out of the box" with our lives and our work, we had no idea, until the day that Mary began moving and speaking through me, that this would be our path.

Robert Dubiel, intuitive counselor and metaphysical teacher, with whom Donald had a conversation back then, suggested that Don and I sit together and meditate for five minutes a day. We were to focus on bringing through the guidance we were seeking, to help us know what we might do with our lives, and so we began. Don had been meditating on and off since he was eleven. At that point in my life, I had no self-discipline for such things, so five minutes seemed doable and non-threatening. I had no idea that those five minutes would completely change my life in every possible way.

As Don and I meditated for the first time, I closed my eyes, asked my mind to quiet, and began to feel the stillness of my body, sensing its weight against the surface on which I was lying. Then, my face started to move about—on its own—wincing, contorting, and stretching. While that seemed a bit odd, I just figured it was part of meditation. After mentioning the experience to Don after we were complete, I learned that, at least for him, such an experience was not typical.

The second time we prepared to meditate, the same movement of my face began immediately, followed by my limbs flailing a bit and strong messages about kinesiology running through my head. While admittedly it was a bit odd to experience, with Don thinking that perhaps I just could not be still for even five minutes for meditation, it all actually seemed quite natural and a bit fascinating to both of us.

The third day when we lay down to meditate again, the movement in my physical body accelerated immediately and I received a strong message to sit up. At that point, I knew the message was not coming *from* me, but instead it was coming *through* me. Being a bit stubborn and needing some confirmation that what was happening was really happening, I responded not by sitting my body up but by saying, "If you want to sit me up, you will have to do it yourself."

Don was distracted from his meditation by all the commotion and sat up to stare at me. To Don, it appeared that there was an invisible string attached to my chest, pulling my body up from the mattress while my arms hung limp on either side of my torso. There were three or four attempts, my body dropping back down to the mattress, until finally, I was in an upright, seated position.

Now, you might want to remember that while we were looking for something a bit different, this was WAY different and yet all truly seemed so natural. It was as if when "They" came through, "They" gave us an instantaneous and innate understanding and peace about the exchange. All I have ever felt when the group of spiritual entities we now refer to as Mary, or the Mary Group, or simply "They" comes through—is pure, beautiful, radiant love.

Once They sat me up, They were off and running, moving about the room on my feet, my knees, and even rolling my body around the floor. Once the movement of my body was figured out, They began to speak with us, offering expansive wisdom, grand insight, and constantly birthing joy for the human experience.

They haven't stopped since. They come whenever we ask and when we don't, sometimes nudge us to let them share something inspiring, affirming, or enlightening. It has been the most magical and transformational journey I can imagine having. Since we first started working with the Marys, They have revealed themselves to us as a group of nine non-physical beings: Mary, Horatio the

Giant, the Director, the Teacher, the Poet, the Ancient One, and three who are unnamed.

Living Mary's Wisdoms and bringing them to the world intrinsically ignites life for Don and me—internally and externally. Each time I shift a thought or belief and feel my life open or I receive a story from another who has felt a complete transformation of something that painfully stagnated his or her life, I feel it would be enough. Yet, there are hundreds of thousands of these moments (countless, really), these stories, these transformations that have come to thousands of those who have received Mary's loving guidance. This book is the resulting compilation of the loving wisdom They have provided. We are so grateful and so excited to share them with you.

—Jacque and Don Nelson

Welcome to this place
where you have always been
where you have never been before.

~Mary

Dear Friend,

We invite you to enter this reading with some measure of belief—or openness to belief—that you are the Creator of your life. Even if it is just one particle of curiosity about the concept of *Living Without Edges* that guided you to open these pages, that is enough.

If you are entering with "convince me" energy, then we would say put this book down for a while until you are ready to receive the gifts offered within these pages and within your life. It is in this understanding of being the Creator of your life that you will experience your true, boundless possibilities.

Through Jacque and Don Nelson, we are joyous to present in these written pages truths, practices, teachings, invitations, understandings, and exchanges that will offer you grand insights into powerfully creating the life you desire to live out loud and to share with your world.

To assist you in creating a smooth and deep journey as you move through these pages, we offer a Glossary of Terms in the back of the book. We have come to recognize that the way we offer some words and phrases may differ from the way they are generally recognized in your world. Also, we offer a differing way of viewing, understanding, and living than may be in your current thought movement.

Our desire is to always offer easily accessible understanding of our insights and teachings.

Edgeless Love,
Mary

Welcome to Me:
Living in a Conscious State of Self-Invitation and Embrace

Imagine waking every day in a chosen state of "welcome." How often, if ever, do you offer yourself the generosity of welcoming yourself to your new day? For instance, when you awake, you could say, "Welcome to me! I welcome me into my life, into my moment, into my breath. I welcome me into my heart, my desire, my passion, my wonder. I welcome me to me!"

We invite you to truly consider bringing this ritual into your full awareness and into your everyday practice of being truly alive. It will allow your passion to fly, instead of simmering just below the bursting point, dulling its ability to ignite you into the full possibility of each new day.

Then take this welcoming of yourself and you into your day. Spread around this open state of invitation, warmth, and valuing of you and others. Open your day, your door, and your heart to life and all that matches you in it. If you would like, go ahead right now and take a moment to breathe in the feeling of "welcome." Feel it spread, sweeping and penetrating, to embrace you and encourage your participation in your own life.

So many humans move from day to day, year to year, without ever really showing up for their own lives. They effectively play bit parts instead of being the main characters in the stories of themselves. We sometimes ask people to imagine themselves standing in a line for their own lives and often, they find that they have put themselves so far back on the list of who is important to them, whose needs they seek to address, whose image of them they need to satisfy, that they can't even see themselves in the line.

By offering yourself the practice of welcoming yourself to your own life every day—in effect, stepping up to the front of the line—you become the main character, well nourished by invitation and value. That is what you will then have to give to all people and all things you encounter throughout your day.

How this truth put into practice changed one life that now offers true change to many others:

Let us tell you a story of a woman who sat in one of our workshops a few years ago listening to this concept of "welcoming the self" into her life. When we offered the image and question of, "Where are you in the line for your life?" her face became very still and her eyes reflected her internal imaging of how far back in that line she might be, and how many characters in her story were ahead of her in her life.

She startled as she realized and announced that she could not even see herself in the line. It was so long and so full that the end of it disappeared into the distance over the horizon. She told the story that she had come to this workshop in hope of receiving insights that would help her to discern why even though her life was full with family and friends and activities, she did not feel fulfilled. She loved, deeply cared for, and was very grateful for all of the people and blessings in her life and yet often found herself wondering why she felt so empty.

In our ensuing conversation with her, we noticed that while she always made herself available and offered love in the best way she knew how, the relationships were often filled with turmoil and drama. She did not recognize that the way she moved with herself and others was actually contributing to her own depletion. Her imbalanced generosity went unseen and unvalued by herself and others.

As we talked, she began to understand that if she was not valuing herself enough to at least see herself *somewhere* in the line for her life, there was not much chance that others would notice her either. Nor would this allow her to have the enriching experience she desired with herself and others. This was a rather mind-blowing realization for her. She had to sit with it for a while.

We were delighted when she continued to engage with us over the course of time in her choosing to continue her welcoming of herself into her day and her decisive moving forward in the line for her life. The more she chose to welcome herself into her moments and the further ahead she got in the line for her life, the more she arrived in her body, and the more she glowed in her own beautiful light.

She reported that her relationships with those she loved were changing and becoming richer. She was feeling more and more satisfaction in her life. She stopped trying to have the right answers for others and instead, began to simply hold space for them while asking them what they felt were the "right" answers for themselves. This encouraged them and empowered them to step forward in the lines for their own lives.

Others started recognizing the wisdom that came from her being centered in herself, instead of her giving them words from a book she had read and tried to apply to their situation, which had been her former practice. She started to find herself thrilled awakening to each new day to discover who she was and how she would move with her life from the front of the line.

After some time, she announced to us, "I got it! All of that giving myself away to other people's issues and difficulties, even though it was done with good intentions and a desire to be helpful, wasn't really helpful at all to affecting change anyway. I was drained and felt very empty. I was getting more and more helpless in my effort to help them because I was disappearing. That is why I didn't feel fulfilled. Like you said, I wasn't in line in my own life. Not anywhere that I could be seen or felt anyway."

Today, this woman breathes her own breath and believes in the ability for those she loves to breathe their own breaths, too. Her heart has regained itself and is opening wide for true receiving and offering because she actually welcomes herself into her own life.

Front of the line.

Question:
What are you doing now?
Answer: Choosing.

Your life experiences are all a matter of choices. Your choices. One of the most impacting and amazing gifts the human has is choice. And yet, we often see so many of you doing anything you can to avoid or deny choice. We find that very peculiar. You really do get to choose how you feel, move, think, believe, and experience yourself in your days.

How are you showing up? What aspects are you choosing to utilize in each moment? Every human is born into the world with the same aspects. Aspects are the treasure chest of self-identifying feelings, moods, sensors, and activators that every human holds within his or her emotional make up. You get them all: Love, Fear, Joy, Wonder, Curiosity, Doubt, Excitement, Trust, Disbelief, Innocence...the list goes on and on. You, as the Creator of your life, choose which of these aspects you hang out with and create through in each moment.

Isn't that wonderful?! In each and every moment of your life, you have access to all of them. However, much of the time, we see you reach for the aspects you use to keep yourself limited, instead of the ones that cause you to move boldly and joyously forward.

For instance, when you are faced with a situation that feels intimidating for you, many of you tend to use the aspects of Retreat, Self-Doubt, and Guardedness, which may appear to temporarily work if you are reacting through a stimulated false fear and a desire to protect yourself. However, calling forth Confidence, Curiosity, and Self-Belief may take you further in the direction of illumination and expansion.

To make a true shift in bringing more well-being into your awareness and experience, it is important for you to recognize that the choices you are making in these situations are either about retreating from the self or moving toward the self. These choices are so much more powerful than anything that is going on outside of you.

You are in a constant state of choosing. There is truly no waking moment when you are not choosing. Consider how powerful this choosing is. You are always in charge of the direction of your thoughts, your will, and your life. Many things will happen around you, because all humans are choosers and Creators. They offer themselves and the other characters in their personal life stories multihued conglomerations of activity and expression. You get to decide how you are going to feel about your moments, move with your life, and become as a result of your experiences.

We often see humans attempting to arrange the parts outside themselves to make it easier for them to feel comfortable in their own lives. This includes attempts to create in other people's experiences by imposing your will on them, or wanting them to be different so it's easier or more comfortable for you to be around them.

We invite you to understand that as you begin to embrace and honor yourself as the Creator of your own life, you will need to relinquish your desire to control other lives.

We assure you, attempting to control others is an exhausting and impossible task anyway. We encourage you to spend your energy, your particles, and yourself, on creating your life instead of focusing on, "If that person would just be different, more loving, more understanding, more open...then I could be happy."

Focus on being loving, understanding, and open with yourself, no matter what anybody else is doing and you will awaken to your own true happiness. Your life and your happiness are yours already. Quit pretending that anybody else has the key to that deliciousness within you or that anything of you is not already yours, instead of separate from you.

If you have convinced yourself that your happiness is separate from you or not available to you, it is imperative that you call it back to your being. Let your happiness fill you to the brim and overflow. Share the overflow with others generously. As long as you are choosing to nurture and feed yourself, sharing yourself will not deplete you.

❦ ❦ ❦

W e would like to share an excerpt from an exchange between an audience member and Mary for illustration.

Audience: How do I stop losing myself to others?

Mary: Stop losing yourself to yourself.

Audience: Can you elaborate on that?

Mary: Of course. Thank you for caring about yourself enough to ask. We are simply saying that the only way you can lose yourself to another is if you have abandoned yourself through practicing some measure of disbelief in you.

Think about it for a minute. Reflect back to a memory of a time you were feeling confident in yourself, allowing yourself to believe in your own heart and your own intelligence, and someone came along and challenged you. Let us know when you have that moment recalled and registered in you.

Audience: Ok, I've got it.

Mary: Good. Now tell us how you responded to the person who was disregarding you.

Audience: How did you know it was about being disregarded?

Mary: We know things. (audience laughs) You gave us permission to come inside you and look around a bit when you offered your inquiry, so we did. Anyway, what was your response?

Audience: I told him he was wrong in his assessment of me and that what I was saying and what I had to offer was valid and important.

Mary: So, in that moment, you knew that you mattered and that you were real? You were actually standing there in your own skin, believing in yourself instead of shrinking or giving yourself away to another, acting as if that person must know more than you do, or simply giving up, believing you will never really be seen or valued anyway.

Audience: I guess I did. I liked it. He still didn't agree with me, but it felt good not to back down.

Mary: It felt good because you did not lose yourself to you and therefore did not lose yourself to him.

Audience: So why can I do that in some situations and not in all situations?

Mary: It is all a matter of what you give yourself permission for, what story you are telling yourself, and what story you are living. When you agree to be there for yourself, you are.

When you have a story inside you that you are agreeing to keep telling yourself such as, "I am not all that bright" or "I don't really know what I am doing" or "I am not enough," that is the energy you show up for yourself with. Change your stories. Change your life.

Audience: Thank you.

Mary: Thank you.

Diversely Living
Your Abundance of Aspects

You cannot give to others that which you have not truly given to yourself first. If you wish to create and experience more goodness in the world, you must first completely open to that goodness within.

Saturate yourself with your own aspects of Love, Joy, Possibility, Trust, Laughter, and so on. Feel the caress of these aspects in their knowing of you and your knowing of them.

All of your aspects are with you to serve you, every one of them. Yes, even Fear, Doubt, Worry, Guilt, and Anger. The trick is to remember that they are *your* aspects. They are part of you; you are not part of them. Therefore, you are in charge and they must take your direction on how they are to serve you.

It's up to you to create a beautiful, honoring, and cohesive relationship with your aspects. These abundant treasures are a powerful part of you. How you move with them is your choice. To help illustrate this concept, imagine a neighborhood with each house representing an aspect. You get to decide if you just do a "drive-by," checking out the houses inhabited by those aspects without stopping to really go in, or if you move in—lock, stock, and barrel.

We watch time and time again as people become willing to move into the houses of Anger or Shame, take everything into these practices of self, all of their belongings, even decorate and try to make it look nice, all the while writhing in desire to escape and move to a different neighborhood.

The only reason you are experiencing the state of writhing, instead of forward movement, is because you have not given yourself permission to move on. Instead, you have chosen to stay right there.

We would suggest that when one of these challenging aspects comes flying forward in you, you look directly at it. Do not shy away or attempt to avoid it, because if it thinks you can't hear it or feel it, it will just get louder.

Instead, have a conversation with that aspect. Learn why it has come. Maybe it's a habit or it wants to offer some form of protection to keep you safe. Tell yourself the truth about why you are experiencing this aspect in its current form and decide if it serves you to continue to do so. You may decide it does. If so, just remember to be in the driver's seat and not to become lost to a renegade aspect running the show.

Always remember that you decide what kind of relationship you will create with each aspect and what role it will play for you, not the other way around.

Did you know that the original intention of the aspect of fear was Authentic Fear? This is a real fear associated with your sense of self-preservation and was simply to be a trigger or catalyst of an internal warning signal. It is with you to let you know that what you are about to do or what you have created yourself into the middle of is perhaps not in your best interest. It may be important for you to change your course of action or inaction. This Authentic Fear's only job is to tell you to trust yourself, to follow your instinct and intuition. It is truly your ally.

Ironically, we repeatedly witness humans ignoring true Self-Preservation Fear, or Authentic Fear. Because humans ignored Authentic Fear, False Fear became a prevalent practice of your internal relationships. False Fear is associated with many other aspects that were also originally intended to be trigger or catalyst aspects, such as Doubt, Mistrust, or Insecurity. When these aspects are practiced through False Fear, they become detrimental stagnations in your life, instead of powerful tools for self-mastery.

Because of its fierce and controlling nature, many believe False Fear to be bigger than they are. Humans then agree to be in a victim relationship with this Fear, allowing it to overwhelm them in their roles as Creators.

We suggest that if this is your current relationship with False Fear, you let it know you are "onto" it. Offer it gratitude for its obsessive commitment to do its job, which was initiated by you in an attempt to feel your safety. In no uncertain terms, let the False Fear know that you are complete in your relationship with it. You are choosing to return to your advantageous relationship with Authentic Fear and its ability to make the hair on the back of your neck stand on end when you need to pay attention. You decide what to do and how to move in the moment. This, too, is your choice, of course.

♥ ♥ ♥

Let us tell you another story to bring this concept home. We were gifted with the grace of meeting a wonderful young woman who came to see us in an attempt to discover why, while she strived daily to find her happiness, it remained illusive to her. She offered that she had studied under many "masters" and fought the good fight to rid herself of all of her negative emotions, and yet, she just could not seem to find her sense of self or a real sense of interest in continuing to live out a life that felt so difficult and empty.

She felt that maybe she was broken and incapable of living as others do. She wondered if maybe she was missing something that others received, which allowed them to feel a sense of connection and ease about their lives.

We listened to her with great interest and offered her our observation that in her attempts to find herself, she was actually throwing herself away. By following the prescription of ridding herself of "negative" aspects, she became more and more depleted and less and less visible. We noted that she was actually disappearing, right in front of us, as she sat there feeling all listless and defeated.

Then we grinned as we encouraged her to invite back all those parts of her she had been swayed to abandon by others. While they had good intentions of helping her, in the end, these instructions left her less instead of more of who she is. We explained to her that instead of running from or rejecting these "negative" parts of herself (which every human has), she may instead just choose to change her relationship with them.

She stared at us a while with a bit of a furrowed brow. We watched as her being's inner workings came to a grinding halt and slowly, yet surely, reversed the direction of her practice of disconnecting with herself. Now they began moving in the direction of embracing and welcoming all of herself back home.

Her expression changed from furrow to grimace in a sort of clenching as she attempted to hold back the avalanche of grief about to unfold. And then the dam broke and her tears breached the rim of her eyes, falling freely down her softening face. As the tears emerged, the light came in. Between her gasps for air, the sounds of wailing moving forth from her became interspersed with laughter.

Her beautiful laughter held within it relief that her now-becoming-former belief that she was broken was dissolving. Her wisdom began to rise from her heart to meet her mind, allowing both to expand into the understanding that there was not one moment, not one particle of her, that was not lovable. Nor was there one part of her that she herself could not love.

In our continued conversation, we assisted her with understanding that when humans remove the Shame associated with their aspects, they free themselves to have relationships with themselves that are pure and full of truth. Shame is an aspect brought into being by humans, and not Creator. (A whole chapter is dedicated to the aspect of Shame. Keep reading.)

We encouraged her to continue her practice of herself in her new-found awareness and suggested that if she were going to "weed" herself in the future, she remove only that which was not of her original being and did not feed her soul, such as old messages, the fears of others, and so on.

We also encouraged her to simply have a conversation with any aspect that made her feel uncomfortable, such as Doubt, and let it know that she was sticking with her choice of happiness. She could choose to tell her aspect of Doubt that it would have to change its relationship with her to support that choice.

Some things are important to doubt; *you* are not one of them.

Living from the Inside Out

Becoming a conscious Creator is very much about living from the inside out, instead of from the outside in. You choose who you are and how you move and how you respond to life. You choose what you offer and what you receive.

If you want to see more Joy in the world, choose to be more joyful. If you want to experience more Love, choose to live from your Love. If you want to have more Opportunity, choose to live through your Belief and Possibility.

On the flip side, if you meet Fear with the aspect of Fear and Sadness with the aspect of Sadness, then that is all you will know. If instead, you meet Fear with Confidence and Trust, and Sadness with Compassion and Love, then you will expand beyond your current internally and externally imposed boundaries to know yourself and your world as edgeless.

You can take this practice of living from the inside out in any direction and into any venue of your life you wish. You may choose your relationships, for instance. By the way, everything is about relationship, which means you are in a constant state of relationship. Be it with your family, friends, work, choices, thoughts, beliefs, wishes, aspects, memories, home, and so on, you are in relationship with everything you encounter.

The wonderful thing is that you get to decide how you move in these relationships—some internal, some external—what you offer to them, what you receive from them, to what degree, and when. It is your life with you in charge. Isn't that delicious?!

If something is feeling out of balance or unfulfilled in your life, explore how you are showing up for your current relationships in these arenas.

Go ahead, dive in. Learn who you are and how you are in relationship with these things. What do you offer? Are you overextended in some areas and negligent in others? It will be important for you to go on this discovery expedition without judgment. Ask yourself lots of questions about yourself and that with which you are in relationship, while not questioning yourself or those things or people. Asking yourself questions and opening to the truthful answers will bring you infinite insight and more and more opening to continued expansive creation.

On the other hand, questioning yourself and people and things outside of you, will bring you limitation in thought and outcome.

To understand the difference between *asking questions* and *questioning*, consider how you feel when somebody is *asking you questions* about yourself or something that you believe in, compared to when somebody is *ques-*

tioning you or something that you believe in. Can you feel the different aspects that rise to be with you in each scenario?

When people are sincerely *asking you questions*, they are inviting you to be seen, to share yourself and your views with them so they may learn and expand with you. When they are *questioning* you, they are challenging you to prove yourself or your beliefs to them. All the while, they are not being genuinely open to what you offer because they have, to some degree, already decided who you are or what they think about what you believe in.

Consider how often you approach life with *question energy* versus *questioning energy*, as delineated above. Choosing to go on this adventure of self-discovery through understanding the nuances and intricacies of your inner workings, through even this one simple distinction—between questioning and asking questions as an example—will be very enlightening. It will offer you great insight into how you choose to explore and identify your experiences through your internal process, and your relationship with your aspects.

❦ ❦ ❦

We are very honored and grateful to be invited into so many lives and to participate with a great variety of soul-opening and life-saturating changes in those lives. We are reflecting, now, on our connection with a particular woman, who came to us demonstrating a rather shy demeanor, head down, eyes deflected, and most always brimming with dampness. Her breath was so shallow and soft that many times, it was almost undetectable as it moved in and out cautiously around the tenderness and heavily restricted freedom of her heart.

And yet, we could see that behind this exterior vibrated a life force so passionate and alive. It seemed miraculous to us that she was able to sustain such a constant practice of attempted invisibility in an endeavor to somehow keep from being crushed by living in captivity, under the command and rules of people and systems around her.

It was her irrepressible curiosity that had survived many "emotional bombings" throughout her life, along with the loving invitation of a friend who helped her find her way to us.

In our first few visits with her, we traveled through much interior and exterior terrain regarding her life circumstances and events. We also explored outside and inside influences from birth to present, and her desire to go into the depths of the pathways of fear she had been traversing. It was important for her to identify her fears and their foundation and to retrieve the moments of her that got lost or denied along the way.

From there, she was able to utilize her Curiosity and her Belief (while somewhat mangled, it was still powerful), along with our encouragement and illuminating insight, began to move our conversations toward what she now chooses to create in her life.

She was able to move from an almost constant state of questioning herself and everybody and everything around her, which always left her feeling trapped, lonely, sad, and afraid, to tapping into more of the passion and aliveness inside her. She formulated questions and explored herself and her life through a chosen state of discovery, and was able to find the answers that arose within her. Answers that led to understanding and more choices of how to move with herself and her life, to gain her sense of self and her possibility. With these choices came vast changes in her demeanor, expression, and practices in her life.

Her previously chosen invisibility was vanishing and being replaced with a demand to be seen and embraced by herself. It was her exterior announcement for all to witness. Her stride became more sure, physically and emotionally. Her vibrancy became irrepressible and she now finds herself living more and more from the inside out. She now chooses how she shows up for her moments, what she does and does not participate in, with her surroundings and relationships, and living her life through her own breath—full on.

All this was complimented by a willingness to own her choices and actions—past, present, and future—and a tenacity to reach in and pull herself out for continued discovery and clearing and opening to the aspect of

More every day of her life. She has very effectively utilized the art of asking questions for the expansion of her existence and to always learn and understand more about the physical and non-physical interplay to bring herself to her most extraordinary experience.

The Stirring Within

We have observed that often, humans feel an Ache, a hunger, stirring inside of them. Sometimes this sensation comes from an unfulfilled space that wants more than it is currently experiencing. Other times, it comes from the excitement and passion of already being in movement and not being willing to go back to standing still for even one more moment of their lives.

If you are experiencing stirring, then you are in some measure stimulating your relationship with the knowing inside you that there is more. Always, always, always more to create, to live, to discover! Your current relationship with this knowing of the constant state of becoming more will determine whether you experience the stirring as an Ache (if you're coming from a Lack mentality), or an excitement for what is to come (if you're coming from a Belief mentality).

Since you are the one who determines your relationship with the stirring, we suggest that you choose to give yourself permission to enjoy it through a state of celebration and gratitude. This choice will feed your momentum toward what it is that you desire to create, never settling for less than the full potential of your experience, of yourself, of your life.

Choose YOU in every moment, moving forward with such a vast heart, so full of possibility, that you begin to witness yourself in a new way. As a result, you begin to witness the world around you in a new way. This is because whatever you are noticing most prevalently about what is occurring in your outside world is a reflection of what you are focusing on and choosing to identify with in your inside world.

Transcript from an interaction with an audience member at an evening gathering with Mary.

Audience: Mary, I am not sure what my question actually is. I think I would like you to help me untangle a tightness I feel inside. Or help me to understand what it is anyway.

Mary: OK. Can you tell us if this is a consistent feeling or if it is triggered in particular situations or environments?

Audience: (pauses to consider) I have to say that it is really almost all of the time.

Mary: (smiling) Well, we have to tell you ... we think you just may have a "stirring."

Audience: A what?

Mary: A stirring. Our friend Donald refers to it as "Suffocating Giant Syndrome." (audience laughs) The interesting thing about this particular syndrome is that you, as the one who carries it, gets to decide if your relationship with it will be a wrestling match, an exchange of oppression, or a catalyzing force of continuous flight with or without a seatbelt in the creation of your life.

Audience: Sounds intriguing. I believe I may have mostly been having the wrestling or oppression experience so far. Can you talk about how I can shift more into the flying with or without a seatbelt plan?

Mary: Sure! You see, this Stirring is actually a very important part of your human experience. It is a very powerful vibrational tool to assure you are always pulsing your life forward and expanding. After all, not one of you actually came here to sit still or simply repeat that which has already been created.

Audience: I can see that. I get bored very easily. It always feels like there is more I could be doing or experiencing or being. But when I look around, I don't see or feel anything that is attracting or really inspiring to me. Sometimes I feel like I might have landed on the wrong planet. Others seem to be content and even get a bit irritated with me for not being content.

Mary: Well, the irritation of others around you not being content is a whole other avenue of discussion. For now, lets just stay on track with your particular Suffocating Giant.

Audience: Sounds good to me.

Mary: Ok. Let's talk about Repeat Energy. We see it as such a devastating practice in your world. We truly do. You see, you are each unique beings with unique ways of thinking, creating, causing, inventing... The idea of all of you coming together is to grow with and through one another. To be the "add" that you are among all of the other "adds" and through your interactions and exchanges always cause more and to birth from that causing, more causing and so on.

Somewhere along the line, because of the energy of Separation, many of you stopped exploring and began making sure you fit within the guidelines of what was already created. Please understand, we are not condemning what has already been created. In itself, it is beautiful.

We are simply inviting you to meet all that has and is already existing and adding your own unique print or idea or self to it as you interact and exchange with the world. Not by bucking against it or feeling confined by it, but instead by inviting it to interact differently with you then it has been experienced before. Even if just slightly differently.

Audience: OK, I feel something moving here. So, I think I get bored easily because I am limiting my own experience of anything and maybe even everything by looking at it as how it already is, instead of how it will be and I will be as a result of me interacting with it. I am not sure if that made sense or not.

Mary: It made perfect sense. You are describing yourself as arriving to exchange with something with the limitation of "it" and you remaining the same as a result of the interaction, instead of you arriving with the idea that as a result of your truly showing up to exchange with its edgeless possibilities anything can happen.

Can you feel the difference it will make when you unsuffocate your giant and let your stirring be about experiencing possibility instead of repressing it?

Audience: Wow! Wow! I feel like my whole self is beginning to split apart at the seems. In a good way. Like I have been seeing and experiencing life through such a narrow view and experience and that is blowing wide open now.

Mary: (smiling) Yes! Yes! For example: Look at this person over here on this side of the room. (*Mary points indicating an audience member.*) Do you know her?

Audience: No, I don't.

Mary: Well, we have to do this fast because your shift is accelerating quickly. When you look at her through your pre-unsuffocated giant eyes, do you see possibility of a whole world of new experiences?

Audience: You are right. I am shifting quickly. I have to look backward in me to find those eyes already. (*laughing*) Through those eyes, I just see a person I don't know.

Mary: Now, release and let yourself move with your shifting that the stirring that is moving without the restraint of repeat is offering you. What do you see?

Audience: I see an unread story. For me. I am sure she has many readers. (*smiling*) I feel an invitation to discover what I will learn about myself by interacting with her.

Mary: Do you now see that in all of the others here also?

Audience: Yes! This room has become the most exciting place of potential, possibility, and discovery that I have ever known. Not that it didn't hold some of that before, but now it is boundless!

Mary: Yes. It is boundless now because you are boundless now. You have set your stirring free to open you to yourself and to life in any given moment. Are you still bored? (*smiling*)

Audience: No! Not at all. I am excited and inspired to live my life this way. I had so been feeling trapped by this stirring somehow. Now I feel fueled by it.

Mary: Yes. And there you have it. Free and alive. Truly alive. No repeating anymore because you will now arrive excited to learn what new you will discover in all things.

Audience: Thank you. Thank you. My life will never be the same.

Mary: (*laughs*) You are welcome. Now, you may irritate others because you are so exuberant instead of because you are bored.

Audience: (*smiling, nodding head*) I am OK with that.

Mary: Good, then. Oh, and by the way, your new eyes will not only notice and be inspired by the "stories" as you stated it, of other people and how they will grow you in discovering yourself more. Your new eyes will also see the same expansion and creation possibility in your exchanges with energies of moments, places, things, and opportunities. Edgeless really.

Audience: Yes, I can feel that already. If I ever feel bored again, I will let it be my wake up call to open my real eyes and see.

Mary: Perfect!

Storm versus Devastation

You are the Creator of your own reality, a reality that may very well differ from that of the person standing next to you. This is why one hundred people can be exposed to the same event or life circumstance and have one hundred slightly and largely differing stories regarding the experience and its resulting impacts. Some people will live in the energy of the Storm and some will live in the energy of the Devastation.

Your movement with any experience is dependent on how you choose to meet the moment. This will always dictate or guide your resulting creation, unless you consciously change it as you move forward. The beautiful thing about this is that even if you have chosen all your life to linger in the Devastation based on what you have been taught, or witnessed in the adults who surrounded you as a child, or even through a space of comfortable familiarity, all it takes to shift into the passionate, raging, moving energy of the Storm is choice. You can choose to meet yourself differently from the inside, moving toward what you do desire, even if it is just with one more particle of this choice than you showed up with yesterday.

Then tomorrow, or five minutes from now, give your new choice one more particle of you and one more and one more, until you tilt the scales and feel your natural momentum of flow toward your desired outcome.

For example, instead of lingering and lamenting in the Devastation of what is no longer available in your constantly and rapidly changing world, you may choose to leap into the "storm" of transformation and unfolding new beginnings. Brand-new moments never experienced before are there, in the Reach—the realm of all Becoming—awaiting your wildest creations, beckoning your movement and invitation to expand beyond anything ever known to your Earth.

As we interact with others, we take great care to offer insights, new perspectives, and tools that can be utilized, if chosen, to cause a change or perhaps a new way of being in your lives. As we were talking with Jacque about her indecision around the timing on leaving her "day job" to release herself fully into the work she is doing with us, she fluctuated many times in her thoughts about what circumstances might warrant her taking the leap. We, as always, would love her through these wrestlings and invite her to search from the inside out to find her answers, instead of determining them based on "circum-stances" outside of her.

One day, she finally asked us for our assistance in finding her way to this knowing space inside. We were quick to suggest to her that she had been hanging her hat on the devastation of excuses, which kept her distracted and unclear about her own internal knowing. With that, we suggested she do what we refer to as "A Dance of Devastation."

The process would require her to write out all the excuses she was clinging to that were holding her hostage from stepping into her own clarity around this subject. Because she asked for our assistance, we informed her that she had 247 of them. Though she could not imagine she had actually developed so many excuses around the subject of "to leave or not to leave or when to leave" her long-standing position as a Human Resource Director for a non-profit organization. The shock of the number moved through her like a lightening bolt. She agreed to let this idea and information register in her and open herself to the "when."

Within a couple of days, she woke in the wee hours of the morning and went immediately to her computer, where she placed her fingers on the keyboard. The listing of excuses commenced rapidly and flowingly. One after the other spilled onto the computer screen and after she tapped out the last one, she counted them and found there to be exactly 247. We will tell you that seven of them in a row were "FEAR!"

Other than that, there were all of her worries, concerns, fears for herself, her family, her financial well-being, and particularly her exposure as one who channels Spirit. She had not yet shared this gift with many others, including her co-workers, her peers, and colleagues in professional groups. Nor did she want to abandon worthwhile projects in which she was involved. On and on, these fears easily identified themselves and spilled onto the list.

When she had completed this part of the process, she was filled with a mix of awe, release, awareness, and excitement—"storming energy." We then directed her to print out all those devastations, cut them into separate pieces and spread them all out on the floor. These were all the things that had been holding her back from giving herself permission to embrace and really live her life passionately with the full-on movement of the storm of Jacque.

Once they were spread out, we had her cue up her favorite power song and play it loudly while she danced on the Devastations of the excuses she had formerly created to hold herself back. With each step, she felt her freedom to choose and her belief in herself and her future growing inside her. By the time the song ended, she leaped out of the pile and into the space where the Devastation didn't exist. Into what was *real* and into what was *reality* in her life. And she knew the time was "now." With that knowing, she released herself into her Confidence, Wisdom, Joy, and Readiness.

She sat down at the computer once again and with great speed, eloquence, and truth, she wrote her very brief, meaningful, and whole letter of resignation. She turned it in that day.

The Weaving and You

You are a unique being. There has never been and will never be an exact replica of you. Just like snowflakes, no two human expressions are identical. You offer a vibration and a gift to the world that nobody else possesses. Once you birth these into the world, they are available for all others to tap into and pull from to augment their own creations. Similarly, everything that every other conscious existence has offered is available for you to resource as desired.

You are never alone. You are a glorious part of the grand Oneness of all that is. You are unique in your expression and vividly blended in your connectivity to the whole, therefore singular and infinite at once.

All things are interconnected in the Weaving, the Grand Choreography that assures that all components fall into place in the perfection of intersections, independent of time and space. There is no separation, except for that which you believe in and cling to in your individual reality. All things are created from Original Source, which is the pulsing of love, pure love, intoxicating and immeasurable in its capacity to know itself through continuous creation.

Whether you refer to this source as God, the Universe, the All That Is, the Great Oneness, Mother, Father...the source of what it is remains the same—INFINITE, EDGELESS LOVE.

That is what you are—in the center and in every particle of your existence. No exceptions. It is up to you how you make this edgeless love that you are evident to yourself and others—or how you choose to make it *not evident*—through the unfolding story of your life. The story you are writing with every breath. It is very important, then, that you become the biggest influence in your own life. That you always choose nothing less than being in the driver's seat of self-creation.

Feel free to invite plenty of passengers (both your aspects and other humans with whom you are in relationship) to ride with you, maybe even to help you map your route. Just remember that in the end, you choose the turns, detours, explorations, and straight-aways by your own design. Oh, and be sure to build in an ejector button for those who won't take "no" for an answer when it comes to creating your life. Set them free to create their own lives.

So then, from the driver's seat, you express a desire and the Universe answers, using the full expanse of the Weaving. We will always give you what you are asking for. You may not always recognize the form in which the answer comes, yet it is always there. When you make a choice to change your life, to move in a more expanded direction, into whatever it is you desire and you move toward it, you are no longer spinning in the illusion of "stuck."

If you want to know what a joyous, blissful, unrestrained life feels like, then dive in and do it really, really well! Depending on where you are starting from in the chosen shift, this causing of activated change in your life may feel like you are expertly driving a well-made sports car around the curves and hills of the open road. It can also feel like you have just seated your inexperienced self behind the wheel of a powerful race car, speeding past the flags, with you grasping to gain the controls of internal self-mastery in an attempt to avoid spinning off the track.

Whatever you choose, move toward it at whatever self-identified pace you select. The trick to success is that you need to be ready to agree to really go. We have watched so many people order their tickets and not get on the ride. Or begin the journey, panic over what they will leave behind, and then attempt to go back.

We offer to you the wisdom that when embarking on significant shifts in your life, give yourself permission to move at a speed that is a match to you in your day-to-day recognition of yourself. Remember to always be your own biggest influence on the speed and pace at which you move. Once you have made a decision (a true, bone-tingling decision), everything you need to support that decision will be offered to you. Be sure to give yourself the presence to pay attention so you are able to recognize the answer.

The Weaving can activate the forthcoming answer in many forms. Perhaps you will notice that new people start appearing in your life who are really fun to be around and really love you for who you are, and you don't feel the judgment you used to feel. Or there may be people falling away from your life who really didn't serve you very well because they were controlling, they were confused, or felt they needed to take more from you than what was really healthy for you to give.

So we say to you: make a decision to start moving your life and be ready for your life to start moving. If the resulting shifting is too big for you in the moment, just pull back a little and adjust the speed of change. This is much more fun and a lot less painful than pressing against restraints while you are launching like a rocket.

Donald has been a wonderful expression of many of our teachings over the years and we take great delight in offering you a little story about one of his experiences that offers a great depiction of the Weaving in action.

Several years ago, shortly after Don and Jacque were married, they attended a weekend-long retreat in Chicago. During this retreat, they had the opportunity to meet several people, among them a young woman named Wendy, with whom Don felt a very easy and enjoyable connection. As the group moved through the weekend, there were several opportunities for discussion and connection. Through this sharing, they learned that Wendy was from New Zealand and at the time, was living in Chicago working as a physical therapist.

At the weekend's wrap-up, they shared e-mails and parted company. Over the years that followed, Jacque and Don thought of Wendy from time to time and wondered how she might be doing and if she still lived in the United States or had moved back to New Zealand or elsewhere. Though curious, they did not make any attempt to contact her.

One day, Don was updating their mailing list of contacts and came across Wendy's information. He decided to include her in the mailing list for sending notifications of upcoming events, even though he had no idea if her information was still accurate.

A week or two later, Don was very happy to take a little trip up to the Apostle Islands and kayak for a few days with two friends. On their last morning out on the vastness of Lake Superior, he and his friends were exploring some sea caves when he saw a group of kayaks approaching. Though he could not yet make out their faces, he slowly began to hear their voices. He and his friends continued to paddle gently in the deep, cold waters and rocked easily though the caves.

When he paddled his kayak toward one member of the group, he heard her accent and asked where she was from. Jokingly, she replied "Chicago." Knowing he had asked because of the accent, she smiled and said, "New Zealand."

Don smiled deeply with a growing knowing and asked what her name was. She replied, "Wendy." It was at that point that his smile became as broad as it could get, and asked, "Madgwick?"

Puzzled, she said, "Yes."

He began to laugh and mentioned the e-mail he had just sent to her without any idea if it would reach her or not. They both engaged in joyful conversation around the chances of meeting out there in the middle of Lake Superior while kayaking, so many years after their initial encounter.

The Weaving does enjoy being clever in how it brings things together. In this instance, Don and Wendy met under the vibration of a very magical weekend, so the reunion was delightfully brought through the same height of feeling and experience. Don was very excited to share his story of the meeting with Jacque when he once again had phone reception.

They have since all formed a wonderful ongoing friendship that has offered much to each of them. That friendship is filled with a deep appreciation for one an- other and for what they can each create when they call Love and Fun and Magic into their lives and then let those aspects find them.

Living in the Absence of Fear, Embracing a Life of Peace and Freedom

L et us begin by discussing what True Fear actually is in its original form. This is the Fear that allows you to know not to step in front of a moving vehicle or not to put your hand on a hot stove. This is the Fear that monitors the safety of your physical being and moves very much in alignment with your self-preservation. True Fear is important. True Fear is a self-preservation stimulator and works very much in line with your intuition and your instinct. It moves with your physical, as well as your non-physical, being.

This is the same original Fear that has the power to alert your "warning system" for your emotions, your mental well-being, and your creating. To ensure the self-preservation of your Joy, your Free, your Expanding, and so on. For some time, we have noticed that humans have the ability, and often practice, the partial or complete ignoring of this true, natural Fear when it comes to emotional or mental well-being. That tingle you feel on the back of your neck or movement in your gut that signals that something is just "not right" for you or with you in a situation.

This True Fear alarm suggests that you might want to withdraw your participation from a relationship or environment or practice. We watch time and time again as this very clear and accurate signal is denied, rejected, or overridden through telling yourself that you must be wrong or crazy to think or feel the way you do. This self-denying often occurs when others don't agree with you about your dismay or don't seem to notice or confirm what it is that has you alerted to something that feels threatening to your well-being.

Humans' ability to question or second-guess themselves or get used to something, making it good enough because it seems reasonable in the eyes of others, is somewhat astounding to us. Of course, the reason you can do this is due to the hypnotism of Separation energy. Separation energy's ability to continue its influence on humanity is dependent on each of you being at least a little bit destabilized, leaving you shaky and uncertain, and therefore vulnerable to mass influence. This destabilizing is also a very good avenue for Separation energy to use its powerful tool of False Fear to suck you into its many enticements and lead you to self-evaporation.

False Fears are a result of "dysfunctional relationships" with one or more of your treasure chest of aspects. The energy of False Fear actually keeps its antenna open and focused on any and all movement of your natural or original Fear, looking for its chance to grab you and lure you into what we call the "False Fear Neighborhood" within your psyche. This False Fear Neighborhood is filled with all of the "houses" that you run into for safety and then get stuck inside of once they have you in a fog or distort your ability to feel and see the self in Truth. These houses do this through all of the misleadings and lies they repeatedly offer to you, leaving you in a weakened state of confusion.

To help you get a better understanding of this concept, let us paint a scene for you. Close your eyes and bring forth the image of a False Fear Neighborhood, consisting of a series of houses, buildings, and various other spaces that hold the energies of such things as Doubt, Anxiousness, and Abandonment, to name but a few aspects. How does this neighborhood look to you? How does it feel? What happens in your body when you hold this image? Perhaps you feel Discomfort, Unsteadiness, a shift in mood. This neighborhood does not have any fences or gates. It is open for you to move into and out of at will. However, it will not tell you this. This neighborhood may even move to make you feel as though there is no exit at all, that you are trapped within it and are destined to live there forever.

As we have had the honor and pleasure of working with many individuals to move their way through and out of this False Fear Neighborhood, we found that many of them began the work feeling as though they really, really would like to have a fence around this neighborhood, to keep what is in there, in. They feared that if there was no barrier to protect them from all of the activity in this well-practiced space within them, they would find themselves consistently either inside the neighborhood again and again, or experiencing the energies of the False Fear "getting out" and trampling their preferred way of being. They believed that having a barrier would allow them to feel safe and free of these influences.

The truth is, the only way humans can really be free is to be free within the self, no matter where they are or what they are encountering. If you attempt to gain your Freedom by being "free from" or "free of" something, the result is temporary at best. This is because your Freedom is then always dependent on what is occurring in your situations, instead of what you are choosing for yourself.

Thus the False Fear Neighborhood remains an "ungated community" for great reason. You see, the goal is to be able to one day stand right in the middle of this neighborhood and know you are always well, because you choose to be your own biggest influence through your whole, ignited, and free relationship with yourself.

You may wonder why you have all of these adverse aspects that live in the False Fear Neighborhood. Why would Creator mess with you like that? You may believe that it would have been better to have only offered aspects that would reflect a world of euphoria. Then perhaps there would be no pain or evil in the world. Here's the deal, though. These aspects, such as the ones listed above—Doubt, Anxiousness, and Abandonment—are not adverse on their own. It was actually the introduction of Shame (an aspect created by humans, not an original aspect of Creator) into your world and life experience that set the course for humans to create these "dysfunctional relationships" with these and almost all other aspects.

For instance, the aspect of Doubt without the tainting of Shame is an important aspect for you. Some things need to be doubted. Some things appear that your True Fear nudges you to investigate further or use your discernment with. The House of Doubt in the False Fear Neighborhood, with Shame woven into all of its texture, is a whole other animal. This Doubt infringes on your Confidence, your Stability, and your Clarity—to name but a few of its impacts. Doubt plus Shame have the power to paralyze your ability to make decisions, to see, hear, or witness things within you and outside of you accurately, and to eclipse you from your own true knowing.

It is the same for Anxiousness. Anxiousness without Shame doesn't leave you Pensive, Uncertain, or Fearful. Anxiousness, in its original form as given by Creator, was to be used as an alert signal, letting you know that there is something to pay close attention to or to have in your awareness so you know what is moving in and around you that may be important to you. To identify things, moments, or actions that are truly unsettling. To give you an opening to see things clearly so you know how to move with yourself and your surroundings with grace and accuracy. This form of Anxiousness can actually be part of growing a trusting and honoring relationship with yourself, allowing you to feel "safe" in your world. Quite the opposite, isn't it?

And Abandonment. You may wonder what could possibly be good about Abandonment. Well, sometimes in life, it is important for you to abandon an idea or way of thinking that is not serving you. Or perhaps to abandon a practice or environment that is draining or depleting you. Abandonment in the False Fear Neighborhood, when mixed with Shame, has a severing effect, leaving you feeling alone and unsupported. Leaving you to believe that you need to hold onto those things that are depleting or draining. Or from another direction, Abandonment mixed with Shame can lead you to feel obligated to remain in a situation that no longer feeds or expands you.

You see, all of your aspects are here to serve you. Somewhere along the line, these aspects got confused in what you signaled them to do to keep you safe. Now you and your aspects are in relationships that do not inspire or feed you. In fact, your relationship with yourself in these houses in the False Fear Neighborhood keep you confined and in a state of practicing yourself as less than who you really are and are capable of being. There is no house in the False Fear Neighborhood that encourages or allows you to be free. Therefore, no house in the False Fear Neighborhood is truly your home.

This does not mean that you do not each live in these houses of False Fear at least some of the time. For many of you, most all of your time is spent in one house or another. You may even believe you feel comfort there. After all, you may see many other people you know in this neighborhood, moving about in and out of these houses along with you. Even though this is true, it does not mean that False Fears are a match to your true self, the self that is free of the tangles of Separation.

You may even be thinking, "Yes, Mary, this is a familiar neighborhood and no matter how bad it can feel sometimes, I learned how to make my life in it and how to socialize in it." We are not arguing with the amazing feats of strength you and so many in your world accomplished by finding a way to spend so much time in the False Fear Neighborhood. You may even feel it is OK, because the time you get to or choose to spend in what we refer to as the "Truth Neighborhood" or "Free Neighborhood" helps to balance that out. Many of you are willing to take the "bad" with the "good."

The Truth Neighborhood, or Free Neighborhood, which is always of Union energy, is filled with houses, structures, open fields, edgeless creations, and possibilities of forms and spaces. These constantly actualize in the free-moving air, brightness, and constant aliveness. This neighborhood offers houses that—along with the true energy of the aspects clarified earlier in this chapter of Doubt, Anxiousness and Abandonment—symbolize aspects such as Love, Celebration, Thriving, and countless more desirable environments for living.

Go ahead, close your eyes again, set yourself free, and call forth your imagining of this place. How do you feel there? Is your heart open? Your mind tantalized? Your breath free? Do you see others here, too? Do you feel like a resident of this space or maybe somebody with a visitor's pass? Do you feel like you can visit and experience this feeling of whole and growing, but need to go back to the other neighborhood to live?

We believe this practice of "visiting" this Truth Neighborhood, instead of choosing to move in and live there, is where statements in your world, like "Too much of a good thing," or "Too much fun," or even "Too good to be true" came from. The resolving of self to the idea that Free, Love, Light, and Airiness can be good to a degree, but then you have to come down from the clouds and deal with the seriousness of life, is a message of Separation. Separation and its permission from you to mingle with your treasure chest of aspects, weaving Shame through them.

So you might wonder why you would ever give such permission to Separation—and what you can do about it now that these dwellings have filled your inner landscape. Well, the answer is: you go in. This time, you go into the False Fear Neighborhood and its many houses, knowing that the only reason you are entering is to reveal the truth to yourself. The truth about all of the falseness and lies these places in you that kept you trapped and tangled. You go inside the False Fear Neighborhood to call all of the moments of yourself that you have lost or given away to these places of False Fear to come back to you, so that you may walk out of these houses whole. In your own choosing. In your own power. You go in this time to leave.

Then close the door gently behind you, knowing that you have chosen for the truth of this house, this dysfunctional relationship you have with this aspect, to be fully revealed to you, and as a result, you have chosen of your own free and powerful will to no longer live in that energy. You can no longer be threatened by the misleadings of this house. Put your hand on the door and declare, when you feel the registration of truth in your statement, "This house is not my home." Walk down the steps, out of the False Fear Neighborhood, and up over the hill into the light-filled inner landscape of true home—the Truth Neighborhood.

Remember, the light-filled Truth Neighborhood represents many of the same aspects as the houses of the False Fear Neighborhood—they are just very, very different here. And you interact with them very differently. This is because they are no longer tainted with Shame and neither are you. Moving into this wonderful, new neighborhood brings with it a whole new internal world to explore and discover from an entirely different positive, powerful friendship with yourself.

So, when we refer to living in the absence of Fear, we are referring to False Fear and all of the lies of Separation, Tangles, and Shame, not your true Natural Fear, which is an aspect to be very much appreciated and listened to. Listened to from Truth, though, not anywhere you visit or live in the "old" neighborhood. And where you can live and embrace a life of Peace and Freedom.

❦ ❦ ❦

We would like to provide you with an example of journeying through and out of the House of Lack in the False Fear Neighborhood:

Mary: As you have made a decision to come into full truth with this House of Lack, where you have lived for some time to one degree or another, we are happy to move with you here and assist you with revealing all of the untruth that has been trapping and condensing you for all these years. We would like to remind you that the difference in this experience with this place today is that you are here through your choosing and the only reason you are going into this house today is to reveal all of its holds on you and to leave it, taking all of you with you when you go. Are you ready?

Audience: Yes. Yes, I am.

Mary: Close your eyes and breathe. Allow yourself to begin forming a picture of this house through the way it has made you feel to live in it. Step inside. Tell us, what do you see?

Audience: There ain't nothing in this house. It is empty. It is a vacuum.

Mary: Yes. (*inhaling and exhaling as they move with this person*) It is a void. A threatening void.

Audience: (*with a tearful gasp*) Yes.

Mary: Yes.

Audience: It is a void that has consumed me.

Mary: Yes. We can see that it is a void that gnaws at you and threatens you every day.

Audience: Yep. It does.

...after a moment to hold an embracing space, Mary continues.

Mary: Tell us. What does it look like in this house. Besides empty?

Audience: Dark...Void.

Mary: Can you find yourself in there?

Audience: No.

Mary: Enveloped by the dark void.

Audience: It annihilates me.

Mary: Yes. We can see that. That is its movement, its message.

Audience: Like I don't exist.

Again breathing together to hold space for processing.

Mary: How long have you lived in this house?

Audience: Ever since I can remember.

Mary: What are some of the messages you feel or hear coming from and through this house?

Audience: I can sense a lot of "can't have," "can't believe," "can't trust" messages bombarding me.

Mary: Yes. Remember that all this house tells you is untrue. It is working to weaken and keep you there.

Audience: It offers a constant state of belief that there is no state of ease. There is no flow. Life is all about suffering and fighting tooth and nail for everything. And every time that anything about money or finances or something that I desire moves in me, it shows up and slaps me. Frightens me. It is an ugly, ugly house. Feels like it is a bottomless pit of not having.

Mary: Again, remember. You are only here today to have the false messages of this house revealed to you and to make the choice
to leave it.

Audience: Yes. I can't see the door because it is so dark. I don't know how I got in here to begin with or how I will get out. There are no windows. It is suffocating.

Mary: Remember, that is the impression it is giving you. You can breathe. Go ahead, take in a full breath and exhale. (*breathes*)
Now another and feel your lungs expand with more ease.

Audience: Thank you. I can breathe now.

Mary: How committed are you to this house?

Audience: Um, I guess I have been very committed, but I am divorcing it.

Mary: (*laughing*) Are you filing?

Audience: I am filing for divorce right NOW.

Mary: It can keep everything, right?

Audience: Yes, Absolutely.

Mary: Everything except for you, right?

Audience: Yes, everything but me.

Mary: And if it refuses to sign the papers?

Audience: Doesn't matter. I am done with it anyway.

Mary: Good, then. Let us take another look around this House of Lack. Just to make sure there is nothing in here that will attempt to convince you to return. Do you see anything?

Audience: A big, black hole.

Mary: Yes. Would you like to step inside it?

Audience: Not really, but I have a feeling I need to anyway.

Mary: It is up to you. However, we are going to ask you to walk through it with us because to truly leave this house, you must allow yourself to not be afraid of it.

Audience: Hmmm, yes, that is true.

Mary: Because when you stop being afraid of it, you will stop believing in it and guess what will happen to it?

Audience: It won't have any hold on me.

Mary: It will cease to be able to make you believe it is real. Yes.

Mary: Would you like to take any aspect or anyone with you for your journey through the house?

Audience: Delight. Possibility. Abundance. Joy. Love. Flow.

(Mary nods and breathes with audience member for a moment.)

Mary: OK, they have all agreed to come. They are saying, "Oh, it is dark in there. What are you going in there for?"

Audience: *(Laughing)* I am sure they are. We can shed some light in the corners...

Mary: So let's use all of these aspects to begin to illuminate the House of Lack. Because it is not really just a big black hole. It has just made you believe that. So, go ahead, begin to shine the lights around and begin to see that this house has a floor and it has walls. It is just a house. It has always been just a house in the neighborhood. And the chains rattling in the dungeon downstairs are just an effect. And the screams from the attic are just actors. It is just a house.

Audience: Feels like the spooky of Halloween.

Mary: Yes. So let's put brighter flood lights in there so that you can clearly see every nook and cranny of it. Every room, every closet, every cabinet.

Audience: It is full of cobwebs.

Mary: It doesn't like to be seen. That weakens its ability to keep you precarious.

Audience: There are a couple of vampires in there, too.

Mary: Yes. Vampires. Creatures who threaten and move against your will to suck you dry and leave you with nothing. Remember, they are an illusion.

Let us continue in our exploration. Oh, and be sure to take some Curiosity with you as you look behind the doors and in the cabinets. Here now, with all of this revealing light shed on it, you can begin to realize that once you can see what is lurking, it is not that frightening. It doesn't have a hold on you any longer. It can't devour you. You can see it. It is just a house.

Audience: It needs some serious redecorating. (*Laughter*)

Mary: Yes. A fixer-upper. It lacks much style.

Audience: Yes.

Mary: So you are going to continue looking through it and as you do, make some decisions about changing your relationship with Lack.

Audience: Yes. Definitely.

Mary: Now that you have put yourself in charge of your experience in this House of Lack, you can see it for what it is. It can't drain you anymore. It can't own you. It can't chew you up and spit you out and it can't threaten you anymore. Because the truth of it will remain illuminated for you. The flood lights will never burn out.

(*Breathing, calming*)

Mary: Look around. Is there anything in this house that you choose or need for your life besides yourself?

Audience: NO.

Mary: Very good. Are you ready to leave it?

Audience: Yes. Yes, I am.

Mary: It is going to be very important for you to make a powerful and real announcement before you leave this house. It is also important that you feel the words of your announcement as true and real for you when you speak them. So let these words, these choices, move around inside of you until you feel their truth for you and then repeat them. OK?

Audience: Yes.

Mary: False Fear Lack, I move from you with Ease and Grace and Light. And, I no longer believe in the power that you had over me.

Audience: (*Pauses, breathes, and repeats the words.*)

Mary: I have no interest in your invitation to stay.

Audience: (*Repeats.*)

Mary: And you are not invited to visit me.

Audience: (*Repeats.*)

Mary: I don't like you. I don't choose you.

Audience: (*Repeats with volume*) I DON"T LIKE YOU! I DON"T CHOOSE YOU!

Mary: Are you able to recognize all the spaces in your life where this burden of Lack has stifled or entrapped you? How your now-former relationship with this house was to carry it with you all the time?

Audience: Yes, I do see all of the ways Lack has burdened and tortured me. And, yes, I did carry it with me constantly. Not anymore. Not anymore...

Mary: Are you ready to leave taking only you with you?

Audience: Yes!

Mary: Good, then. Look across the room. Do you see the door?

Audience: Yes. It is clear to me.

Mary: Go on over and walk out through it. And, close it gently behind you. Pause for a moment there on the porch. Breathe your breath ... And turn and put your hand on the door and repeat these words when you are ready: "This house is not my home."

Audience: (*nodding, pausing, now smiling*) "This house is NOT my home."

Mary continued with the audience member as together they walked out of the False Fear Neighborhood and out into the new neighborhood, the Truth Neighborhood. The new Neighborhood holds all kinds of very different feeling houses, including a House of Lack. However, in this house, there is a Lack of Worry, Lack of Self-Punishment, Lack of anything that holds us each separate from our most whole, connected selves.

Choosing Your Own Flight and Flight Pattern

People will say to us, "I want to fly a hundred million miles an hour and I really want to use my wings and I really want to go full-on into my unexplored life, but I want to take all these things and people with me."

Guess what? A lot of those things and people don't desire to fly as fast as you and are never going to.

The hardest thing for people to release in practicing the concept of causing real change in their lives is other people. You want to take your friend with you and you know that your friend is usually in a place of Indecision, Lack, and Doubt, but you really love your friend, and you would like to take the friend with you because you think it would be really good for the friend. We understand your beautiful intention with this idea and yet, in truth, you are trying to create in your friend's experience. So what you have to move to is getting into a space of giving yourself permission to fly at your own speed, and to find out who and what goes with you.

Do not attempt to predetermine these things, because if you look inside all those bags you're trying to carry with you, you'll likely find out that you are holding onto most of them for safety. Really, there is not going to be a lot of use for them when you get to where you're going anyway, because "there" is not going to be about being safe. You can go there and be sure, confident, powerful, expansive, in your natural and craved state of well-being.

We know safety is a huge issue in the human experience and that it is very important to you to feel safe. However, there is a big difference between not feeling safe from the False Fear space, and feeling safe from a space of certainty, an expansive and wisdom-filled space, a known space of your true well-being.

So we would say, start working toward being willing to fly without concerning yourself with where you are going exactly or how you will get there. We know this idea can feel tricky and yet, as long as you are moving in the direction of your desires, you need to decide to fly and go anyway if you are to chart your own course and create your own way to your chosen destinations.

You can always invite company. Willing, ready company.

"I can't do that. My whole life will change!"

We often meet with people who tell us long, beautiful, intricate stories of their lives and offer expressions of great desire for things to change. When we move with them and offer clear insight to openings and possibilities that exist within them as a result of their expressed desires, which would surely change the current course of their lives, they say, "I can't do those things. My whole life will change."

(We marvel at how often humans leave us completely baffled and yet, we are constantly falling more and more deeply in love with you.)

This exasperated statement of "My whole life will change" is usually followed with many weavings of wonderfully imaginative excuses as to why it is not possible for them to make the suggested changes. In other words, they offer us more proof of their current state of Devastation. We wonder if they were willing to let the Storm of Desire strip away all their excuses and defensiveness, what would be left to guide them?

The truth, of course.

Years ago, a woman came to us, seeking. She stated she did not know what she was seeking, but something had to change in her life. She could feel herself slipping away, slowly drowning in a life that didn't fit her and left her joyless. She said she had all the things that offered the image of "the dream"—a spouse, children, a home, a good job and yet, every day felt like a struggle to wake into and live. At the end of the day, emptiness was her more constant companion. She talked of the migraine headaches that plagued her and the exhaustion that filled her body and mind, leaving her feeling disconnected from her experiences—the ones that felt good and even the ones that felt bad. She just wanted to run away. We listened intently to the ins and outs of her life situation, details, and contemplations. We held the space for the telling of the perils of her attempts to reach for and choose something that felt like life to her.

When she was finished offering her story and giving us a character description of the many people who filled her days, we asked her one question: "What role do you play in your story?"

We continued, "Other than telling us the outcome of how you are feeling in your body as a result of the many circumstances of your life, we haven't really heard much about you at all. You have told us a story of who you *aren't*, instead of one of who you are. No wonder you wish to run away. You are attempting to live in a life that is yours, but for which you are not there. Not in any meaningful way to yourself anyway."

She just sat for a few moments, staring at us, assessing what we had said, and then the tears streamed easily.

"There you go," we said, "You just showed up. Welcome back to you."

We went on to talk about what it all meant and had several conversations as the days and weeks unfolded, beginning with and moving through the resistances she had to being an important person in her life.

Our suggestion is always to be the most important person in your life because it benefits everybody.

We recommended finding some pinhole openings— some tiny changes—to actually make decisions that would move her out of her undesirable state of existence. All the while, she argued over and over again, "I can't do that; my whole life will change."

Simultaneously, she was begging for a way to change her whole life. She wanted desperately to experience a full-out self-emancipation from the internal pain prisons in which she had kept herself by not giving herself permission to make choices that counted her in the mix. These were the causes of the migraines and exhaustion.

As we worked together, her physical, mental, emotional, and spiritual expressions of self shifted and changed. She felt her true freedom from bondage for perhaps the first time in her life. She was now making choices that came from love and offered so much to herself and others. She was happy.

And then she ran into some "speed bumps" with those around her who believed they needed her to go back to the way she was before. They told her stories of how they would change if she would just keep things the way they were. That they would be more caring and loving and available. That they just needed her to pull herself back in and think of them and care for them and make them feel comfortable. That their years of disregard for her would be put in the past and everything would change.

And, so, she said "yes" to them and very effectively said "no" to herself. She really believed she could do it, that she could just tuck back inside and find a way to be happy by serving them. She convinced herself to believe their words, although their actions did not match those words. It didn't take long before she felt ten times worse than she had before she ever came to us.

One day, she pulled herself up from her desolate state and came to see us again. It was then that we looked at her with complete and utter love and said, "We understand completely. It is very painful for a butterfly to attempt to climb back into its cocoon."

Again, she stared at us for a while and cried. This time, though, she feared she had killed the butterfly. We assured her that she had not, that the butterfly was still fully alive. That was the part of her that brought her to us. She offered that the truth for her was that she did not know if she could do it again. That she would have to take time to consider the possibility of re-emergence and wait until she knew she could do it before she gave herself to her own life—the life "safely" hidden inside of her again. We told her we would never leave her side.

One year later, she found her way back. She was choosing between her life and death and she had chosen life, no matter what it was going to take. She allowed movement for releases of grief so deep she thought it might kill her to let it go. She reported she had never cried so much and for so long in her life. We let her know that it was a lifetime of repressed tears now given their allowing and freedom.

She marched through false fears and confusions that had formerly kept her suppressed and confused. She declared herself as a life worth being lived and shared and whole. And from there, she made her choices and stuck to them—all through love, no matter what came back at her. She still hits rough patches, but knows they won't own her because now, she owns herself.

And she still has children and a home and a job and now herself and all of the love and aliveness that that brings with it.

"Shoulds" and Other Well-Written Fiction

How often do you tell yourself the truth about yourself? We watch humans most consistently and constantly assessing what they believe to be the truth about others. They feel as though they have clear insight into what others are hiding from or denying and yet, they very seldom play in their own yard when it comes to this activity.

We recognize that this can come from the greatest loving intent to care about others and offer solutions to those "in need." Yet, this "taking care of" others usually ends with sometimes uninvited assistance, laced with many "shoulds," both spoken and inferred. And to add further complication, "shoulds" almost always trigger fiction writing in the person at which they are being hurled, even if it is you hurling it at yourself.

Something about this "should" energy causes the human mind to immediately assume more is going on than what is being addressed. Now you are off to the races with the spinning of all kinds of internal tales. Such stories can sometimes become very difficult to even track back to the original "should." Once imagined, these stories threaten to act more as memories (even though in reality, they are false memories) or assessments of the situation or the person involved, than the truth does.

We ask you: When was the last time you were "should" on and enjoyed it? We would guess never. And even so, "shoulding" on others and yourself is an activity that seems to consume much time and energy in your world.

We have had some fun inviting friends to keep a hash mark count on a little index card of how many times they experienced "should" energy in a day. In other words, they were to keep track of how many times they felt "should" energy coming from within or from the outside in, aimed at themselves or others from another.

The practice of "shoulding," both consciously and unconsciously, is rather rampant, so if you choose to take this challenge, carry a rather large index card with you to keep the tally. Especially if you include all that you read and hear in the background noises of life. One political discussion, for instance, may fill up your card completely. Or for some of you, one conversation with a controlling friend, family member, or workmate would do the trick Oh, or maybe just in one critical conversation you have with yourself may do so. Whew, that's not always an easy one to accept, is it?

However, if you are telling yourself the truth, unless you somehow completely escaped the negative and fearful forces of the world, at some point in your life, if not now, you will feel some familiarity with this practice. You see, "shoulds" always come partnered with the aspects of Obligation, Expectation, Force/Control, and often False Fear. Not the most attractive energies to have flying at you, whether from the inside or the outside.

When you are hurling the "should" at another, a correct or incorrect response supported by well-written fiction in your judgment, is already predetermined within you. This really limits the opportunity for either one of you to shine from the exchange, unless it is in the illusion of satisfaction in triumph over another. Yes, it does offer opportunity for each of you to force your will or strength of opinion upon one another, and yet, one of you will always end up feeling coerced through Guilt or another well-wielded aspect.

If the coercion does not work, one of you may feel disappointed in the other's unwillingness to adhere to the expressed, believed-in best interest for that person. So, because we know that it is the rare human who is truly desiring to mistreat or dim the light of another whom they love, the practice of "shoulding" is something learned and done out of habit, and usually not out of malice. Nevertheless, the result remains the same.

If you wish to arrest this potentially fracturing practice, we suggest you take a look at what is behind the "should," whether you are the one dishing it out or taking it in. We give this example of a possible communication with your child to assist you in understanding:

"It is well after midnight. You should have called. I had no idea where you were. You should be more thoughtful and respectful of me and the rules we have in this house." (These words are usually spoken with much passion, followed by a threatened or implemented consequence.)

What is really being said is, "I get so scared when I don't know where you are or if you are safe. The love I have for you is so immense that the thought of anything happening to you is more than I can bear to think about. I need you to honor me and the rules we have set in this family to let me know what is going on when the planned schedule changes unexpectedly so I can breathe."

The first example is a reprimand and recognition of the child's failure to meet your expectations. The other is an invitation for the child to feel your heart and know why a simple phone call is so important to you and your mutually honoring relationship. The former is delivered through fear. The latter is delivered through love. Both can offer consequences as a result. It is just that the one delivered through love will have a much more truthful, meaningful, connected, and long-lasting resonance that truly changes things between you and your child for the better, than the one delivered through fear.

Even when "should" is used in an encouraging fashion, like, "Oh, yes, you should do that! You should take the risk and go for it, you really should!" it may feel like a push from the outside in. It is as if you are attempting to strongly influence another's decision through forcing an override of his or her own discernment, doubt, or hesitation or perhaps the other's own inner knowing and natural timetable of readiness.

Instead, you may wish to listen and express your support in a state of celebration and belief in the person you are encouraging, like, "I can see how excited you get when you talk about this possibility. I can feel your pure flow kick in and I am very excited for you in whatever you decide to create with it in your own good timing. I will be right there with you, cheering all the way if you choose to do it." This response conveys your trust and belief in the other person and your recognition of his or her ability to know what and when something is a good match.

People want to be seen, believed in, and received. That is inherent. Another example may include an exchange with an intimate partner: "You should be different than you are." Translation: "I want to feel more safe and excited in our love for one another. I desire more mutual valuing and cherishing of one another in our relationship." One is a demand to change something about the other that you deem wrong and that can most likely not be completely satisfied, even if your partner is inclined to attempt to do so. The other is an invitation to move toward a mutually beneficial outcome.

"Shoulds" tend to garner the responses of either throwing up shields or delving into a dose of guilt for those at whom they are tossed. This is because people tend to either not feel seen or to question themselves and dive into defensiveness or devaluing of the self when this "should" energy is present. These responses will call forth Resistance, Resentment, and sometimes even feelings of Betrayal of trust in varying measures. There are even the occasions when Apathy is the chosen response, which is the state of complete disconnection.

This is true whether the "should" is internal or external. So, you see, releasing yourself and your world from "should" and replacing it with Invitation and Truth will be a highly transformational experience in your life, and therefore your world.

❦ ❦ ❦

We were enjoying a rather fascinating exchange with a woman a while back, which offered us opportunity to observe just how tightly humans hold onto their "shoulds." She is a long-time and beautiful acquaintance who tells us often of how much she enjoys and expands from interactions with us, and yet, she has no interest or belief in our teachings around "shoulds." We know that the reason for this rejection of the topic is because it is an invitation for her and others to give up utilizing control in association with people and things outside of themselves.

When we offered this insight to her, she crossed her arms and crinkled her brow and let us know that she felt very justified in operating herself through "should," and actually believes it would be a bit of a disaster to be without "shoulds" in the world.

When she announced this to us, we just grinned and said, "OK, we have no investment in whether you keep your 'shoulding' or being 'shoulded' in practice in your life or not. You are free to do as you will. Anything and everything we offer is for you to choose from to apply or not to apply to your creating."

She said she was great with that and began to move the conversation onto other topics and then, as much as it frustrated her to do so, came back to the subject of "shoulds." She is a wonderful, tenacious woman who does not like to leave any stone unturned. It seemed that being given recognition that she was the one in charge and she got to choose what was explored further and what was not, left her feeling like maybe there was something here that she might somehow be missing. We grinned and joyfully opened the conversation to identify what it was about her position on "should" that now felt like it was holding her back. She asked us how "should" was associated with control, and didn't we think that some things needed to be controlled?

We offered to her what we know to be true. The aspect of Control that is part of every human was originally meant to only be used internally to support Self-mastery. It was actually when humans began using Control externally to cause or attempt to cause a shift in behavior in somebody else that disease was introduced to the human experience. This revelation made her pause and draw in a deep breath. This was followed by her tilting her head just a bit and saying, "Really?"

She found this very fascinating and wanted to understand how "shoulds" are tied in with Control. We asked her how she could not recognize the link. We then had her bring up several scenarios in which she felt "should" was not controlling, and each one fell apart as we discussed them. She began to laugh and shake her head. She said she felt "busted." She was having a huge "ah-ah" as she flashed though a variety of moments that included "should" energy she had offered outward, had come toward her, or she had cast at herself.

Our friend could clearly see that no matter what the reaction, even if the "should" was taken in and the person made changes because of it, there was oppressive feeling in the result, rather than a feeling of freedom. She laughed and said that even when it helps her to get her own way, it doesn't feel completely good, as if something important got missed. We told her that what was missing were the feelings of Invitation, Acceptance, and Love.

No real connection is made through a "should," ever. She found herself agreeing and accepted our invitation to release herself from the disconnect that "shoulds" offer.

Once in a while, she still offers herself "should" energy, just to try it out and to intentionally attempt to manipulate something or someone in her favor. She does it with full awareness, though, and usually cuts herself off from this choice midstream. Instead, she admits what she was doing and adjusts herself to just ask for what she really wants.

True Invitation and Choosing

Let us speak of the energy of invitation, pure invitation, that is not laced with expectation or obligation. Invitation that is edgeless in its opening and willingness to recognize what is important in the self and in another. Profound in its ability to welcome true exchange and sharing of layers of connectedness in relationship and exploration of life.

How often do you have your invitation energy cranking in its pure form? Really cranking? Unguarded, unassuming, unjaded. Open and dancing in true innocence and edgeless possibility. Has it been a while? Do you need to dust it off? Or is it right there with you every day when you awaken to the new sun rising? Yowsa!

This begs the question, "What will I bring to this new day? This day unencumbered by the weight of my past and instead, winged with the flight of my moment-to-moment creation. I reach forth into it with my zest and open invitation for the eruption of love and discovery. I invite the me that is in everything I encounter to meet me and charge me with so much matched vibration that my overflow of 'alive' gets on everything in all existence and offers to it all that is desired and fulfilled."

That has got to feel better than the popular "another day, another dollar" approach currently existing in your world. Remember always that you are a chooser and that you are constantly choosing.

Question: *What are you doing now?*

Answer: CHOOSING!

We have had some fun offering the practice of having you write this question on several index cards and placing them in several places that draw your attention in your life—various places in your home, your car, your workplace, your clothing, and so on. They act as triggers to remind you that you are constantly choosing and your choices in every space of your internal and external worlds form your life, created and choreographed by you.

We are not suggesting that you must create a life that is always in its every moment pumped up with zest and zeal, or perfect peace, or love without conflict. We know that you are on Earth to be human and that as a human, you are packed with aspects and emotions and filters that offer you infinite combinations to create your rich and diversified experience.

We suggest that you choose to utilize all or as many of your aspects as you can within your lifetime. We are offering you the invitation to activate them with passion and purpose and to remind you that when you are availing yourself to them, you can use them thoroughly and precisely with the skill of a seasoned director of your own life.

❦ ❦ ❦

Showing Up

As you are moving through the pleasures and challenges of your life, be sure to remember to show up for the experience full on. Even if you are finding yourself to be Ornery and Cantankerous or Doubtful and Hopeless, be *really good* at it. Dive in. Let yourself feel it in every cell. Drink it in. Spend as much time as you want to there and then, move on.

That's the trick: "*Move on!*"

What you will learn as you begin to truly create your life in alignment with your desires—unless Misery and Separation are what you desire (some of you do and we find that to be a perfectly beautiful and expanding creation that fills the world with options and discovery as well)—you will find that you will spend less and less time in thoughts and practices that hold you separate from your love for yourself and others.

Most of you will simply find that it is no longer as alluring or worth it to you to spend your time and energy in moods and ways of living yourself that are contrary to your desire to be Happy or Peaceful. It doesn't mean you will release aspects such as Ornery or Cantankerous from your treasure chest. They are yours, after all, and they are there to serve you when called on. You may just call on those aspects less often or require their participation for shorter and shorter durations. Or perhaps you call on them to offer you assistance in different ways than your previous relationship with them has required in your creation of your life.

Spending less time with Ornery or Cantankerous, for instance, will release you and give you more time to call forth other aspects, such as Delight, Curiosity, Passion, Trust, Exploration, and so on, to move with you in your days.

You are the Creator of your moment-to-moment experiences. You choose how you show up for your exchanges, what you do with what is offered to you, and what you offer to yourself and others every minute of your life. Your possibilities created through choices are as infinite as you give yourself permission for them to be.

❦ ❦ ❦

Audience: Mary, I just want to be happy. Can you help me to get my life to cooperate with that?

Mary: (*smiling*) What are you willing to give up to have your Happiness?

Audience: (*a little miffed at the question*) I don't think I should have to give up anything. Can't I just choose it and have it?

Mary: How are you feeling right now?

Audience: I don't know. A little agitated, I guess.

Mary: Ha! And perhaps there is some Stubbornness and Entitlement running around in there, too?

Audience: Boy, I really don't want to say "yes" to that, but you are probably right. And I suppose a few other not-so-attractive things, also.

Mary: (*smiling*) So, would you be willing to give up your current relationship with these default aspects to experience your happiness more consistently?

Audience: (*now smiling, too*) Oh, I get it. Yes, I suppose I would. I would also be willing to give up Doubt, Worry, Disgrace, Lack...

Mary: Now, don't get carried away. Please note that we asked if you were willing to change your relationship with these aspects, not give them up. Remember, you never want to give any part of yourself away. Giving parts of yourself away is what caused these aspects to be your default response in the first place.

Audience: I guess that makes sense. So how do I change my relationship with my current default aspects and create new relationships with my other aspects like Happiness, Peace, and maybe even Fulfilled?

Mary: You choose.

Audience: I need a little more direction than that.

Mary: Of course. You begin by observing yourself and noticing when you feel good and when you don't. And, you take full responsibility for how you are feeling and what of yourself you are choosing to practice in any given moment.

So, what we are saying is that it is not about observing what is going on outside you, it is about observing what is going on inside you. As you do this, you will become more and more familiar with yourself as a chooser. (*Audience member furrows her brow.*) You may argue with us now and say, "I don't choose how I react to people and things in my environment; it just happens." And, we would just say "OK."

We are not here to argue with you or deny or judge your chosen stories in your life. We are here to offer you insight and truth and you can do with it whatever you wish. Our love remains whole and consistent for you. We thrill in everything you do, whether it is keeping yourself stagnant or launching yourself forward in inspiration.

Audience: No, I think I am getting it. I am listening. I am willing to give up my Resistance for Happiness. (*smiling*)

Mary: Good. So where does your reaction to our outside stimulus come from?

Audience: Me, I am guessing.

Mary: Yes! And it is when you begin to become a keen observer of yourself that you begin to become aware of what aspects, thoughts, beliefs, filters, and practices you have had in place over the years. You begin to recognize if they lean you toward Happiness or away from Happiness.

You must be very honest with yourself about this—no excuses or justifications—just the truth of if your current relationship with this aspect brings you into association with Happiness or not. And then you choose whether or not this practice stays, gets modified, or takes a vacation.

Audience: Do I really have that capability?

Mary: Yes, you do! You have to remember that all of your aspects are with you to serve you and they belong to you; you do not belong to them. So no matter how big and ominous an aspect feels, you need to remember you are bigger than it, because it lives inside you; you do not live inside it. Though we do see many of you move in, deco-rate, and invite friends over to your houses of Worry, Judgment, Struggle, and so on. ***Stop it!*** (*Smiling. Audience members shake heads in agreement and laugh.*)

Audience: Wow! I have to tell you, I never thought of my feelings, my aspects, as characters that live inside me. So to change my relationship with myself and live more Hap-piness, I will have to modify my relationships with all of my aspects to match that.

Mary: Yes! Congratulations! You got it. And practice a lot until it just becomes natural for you to reach for and live an aspect that inspires you, instead of depletes you.

Audience: Thank you, Mary. Really, thank you!

Mary: You are most welcome.

Truth

We have talked with many who say, "I like what you are saying, Mary, and I would really like to create my life the way you say I can, but the circumstances in my life just don't support it."

Pay attention to the stories you are telling. We find it remarkable how willing people are to keep repeating stories fraught with drama and unfulfilling endings. How ready they are to repeat over and over again the same tragic tales of how life is not on their side, blah, blah, blah. "It's so hard." How many times are you really willing to repeat that line? You can write it over and over again your whole life if you choose to.

We have to ask you, "Why would you choose to? How does it serve you?" It must serve you. You wouldn't do it if it didn't. No humans ever do anything that does not serve them in some way. Even when the outside evidence does not appear to be in any way beneficial, humans are always in cahoots with themselves, always working on their own behalf, so such a declaration is supporting something they are clinging to or dedicated to internally.

Oh, and did we tell you that the answer, "I don't know" isn't an option? It isn't the truth if it is about you. "I don't know" is a great answer if it is about somebody else or something outside you, because chances are, you don't know completely, at least not as well as others know themselves.

We are talking about you, though. Why do you do what you do? Why do you think what you think? Why do you move as you do or believe as you do or choose as you do? It is so important— imperative, actually—if you are really choosing to step into Self-mastery and create the life you desire that you answer these and all self-directed questions by telling yourself the Truth, always, one hundred percent of the time. At least earnestly attempt to always provide yourself with the greatest degree of Truth about you that you can find in any given moment.

We know that always telling yourself the Truth is a tall order, a taller order than you might believe at the onset of the task. We know the result of it is what you might consider miraculous in how it will assist you in moving and transforming your life. Even if all you can summon of your Truth is one particle at a time, offer yourself the gift of diving into it this way, until little by little, match by match, epiphany by epiphany, you begin to recognize this Truth as your own.

Yes, sometimes you have buried your Truth or your self-awareness so deeply or been estranged from it for so long that it is no longer remotely familiar to you. That is just the Truth. Keep going. It is time for you to own your life, every particle of it. No more excuses. Your life is in your hands. Your beautiful sculptor's hands that possess innate wisdom and knowing of exactly how to mold and bend and manipulate the clay of your life to create the most extraordinary and uncommon work of art that is you. You as offered to the world from the inside out.

It is not the circumstances of your life that create you. It is *how* you create, move with, and respond to the circumstances of your life that create you in your life. This is evidenced over and over again in your world as you witness individuals who perhaps were raised in very similar circumstances or who have encountered a parallel situation or event in their lives and have moved their lives very differently as a result of those experiences.

How powerful it is to choose to take your life into your own hands and decide how you are going to spend it. To own it and all that you create with it, even the parts that you would rather not take responsibility for, the parts that don't look or feel pretty. Just think how freeing it will be when you can look at the messiest parts of your life and instead of holding yourself in judgment, you say, "Wow, if I could create that, I can create anything!"

In that moment, you begin to move toward yourself instead of away from yourself. You begin to feel the power of telling yourself the Truth without Judgment. "I have made some interesting choices in my life that have resulted in a lot of pain for myself and for other people. That is just the Truth." "In my own assessment, I have really screwed up and done things that I am not proud of, things I would like to be able to erase from my past. That is just the Truth." Once you speak these things out loud to yourself, you are no longer in Hiding energy. You are no longer threatened by those things. They can't spring out and attack you when you least expect it and the energy they once held just fades away. You have looked them in the eye, admitted the Truth to yourself, and now you stand in the powerful position of a "choice point."

When you allow the opening within you to drink in the gift of, "It's just the Truth," you get to look at it without Judgment, Shame, and Fear, and make a choice about how you will move forward from there. When you meet something with the energy of Truth, you have an edgeless force of Possibility moving with you. You may move forward in a very different way, never clinging to the same old excuses as to why you did what you did and therefore completely changing the course of your life. Or you may decide to continue along the same path, holding to its familiarity, or shift a little at a time, putting your toe in to test the waters of change.

Whatever you choose, it is your life to create and to live and to experience and express yourself in, in your very own unique way.

Truth

❦ ❦ ❦

Some time ago, a woman came to one of our introductory evenings for the first time. She entered the room displaying an outwardly chipper attitude, though we felt there was an overriding restriction within her. She chose a seat in the back corner of the room so as not to be too imposing or visible in the room. She sat quietly, listening intently as we spoke—with a rather excited eagerness to inhale everything that was exchanged—as we offered our welcoming, and then as each audience question was posed and each exploration and response was offered.

It was evident that the woman was breathing in every word and attempting to source it into herself. After the evening was complete, she approached Jacque, almost beside herself in excitement for what she had heard. She said that she learned about us and while we were scheduled to come to her city in a couple of weeks, she knew that waiting any longer to find her sense of self and life was not an option, so she got in her car and drove to this site. She was gushing her gratitude for the information and insights she had received, as she felt it all really hit home, knew she was in the right place at the right time, and would continue to interact with us until she had uncovered everything we had to offer.

Since that time, we have had the pleasure of knowing this radiant and remarkable woman as she explored every possible particle of her internal world and came to life in finding a true sense of loving herself. This exploration and transformation was made possible through her tenacious and driven desire to reach inside, tell herself the Truth about everything, own every moment of her life, and pull herself out.

It wasn't long before she was not sitting in the back of the room anymore and instead, sitting in the front. Well, we aren't sure it is sitting so much as bouncing, not just listening, but also asking questions and sharing experiences and new-found wisdom and announcing in front of rooms full of people, "I LOVE MYSELF!"

Her humor has shifted from self-deprecating (defense mechanism) to joyfully entertaining and smart, and her life-long wrestling with her body has become a loving relationship that has shifted everything about the way she eats and moves, even allowing her to reverse some serious diseases that had crept in to take up residency in the once-fertile environment for such things.

All it took was a willingness to do whatever it took to tell herself the Truth about everything within her and to make powerful choices around those discoveries. She will tell you that it wasn't the easiest path to self-realization and yet, she also admits that it felt a lot better than the path to self-destruction that she had been on.

And she wouldn't give up a minute of it now.

Living Your "YES!"

This is your life. Do you get that yet? You are here for this experience for what is a fleeting moment in the continuum of all existence and it is so rich and so real and so full of possibility of all that you can come up with to desire. You get to create. You get to hold the brush or the pen, or the space of wonder or imagining, and cause its movement. You get to decide, decide and choose, constantly...*constantly*... what you create into your experience. Who you are, how you meet yourself, and how you bring yourself to the world. Isn't that fantastic?!

We invite you to live all your moments, all your days, living in the embrace of your "yes." When you say "Yes, this is me, rich in the expression of who I am creating right now," it is GOOD. It is SOOOOOO GOOD!

We are having some fun intentionally stirring up a remembering in you that there is no dull moment unless you choose it to be dull, never an un-experienced possibility unless you choose to overlook it or decline it. Your life is always rich and always full of potential and possibility and you are in the driver's seat. We, of course, are ecstatic to offer ourselves as a GPS to support your IGS (internal guidance system) as requested by you along the way.

If you ask for something and we bring it to you and you miss it, don't worry. We will find another way and another way and another way until you grasp it. We are infinitely clever, resourceful, and dedicated. So there is no need to spend any of your energy worrying about missing a "sign" or an answer or guidance. We are diligent and tenacious.

That being said, we would also like to address the matter that it is *your* dream, and we are willing to support and provide assistance for whatever you choose. However, we will not be in the driver's seat. We have told you before: that is your place in this adventure.

You must live the energy of your dream, feed yourself with it, offer yourself to it completely, and believe in it with all your might. A trick to this is remembering that while most people believe the dream is about something outside of them— something we would call a "detail"— the dream is actually always about the inside result of manifesting the dream.

For example, you may say to us, "I would really, really like to own and drive a BMW convertible. I have been looking at BMW convertibles for a long time now and I can just feel myself behind the wheel." And we would ask you, "Why would having this satisfy you?" It is very important to know the answer to this question within you. You may say, "I want to feel the freedom of driving down the road with my hair blowing in the wind, while I hug the corners with great precision, traveling along at a rate of speed that just slightly pushes the edges of safety, while feeling completely confident in my skill and the car's ability to meet the challenge."

We say, "That sounds perfectly matched to you. Would you be willing to open up to a manifestation that matches this desire, while perhaps presenting itself in a different form, or are you set on the BMW?"

Whatever your answer is, that is fine. We just need to know if you are working with a narrow straw or a grand open space when it comes to satisfying your desire. You see, we are clearly aware that you want so much more than a BMW. You wish to create a life that feels free and full of your own permission to let your hair down and push yourself just past the limits of guaranteed safety (offering you a little life-giving exhilaration), living through your unshakable confidence and belief in yourself to handle the curves of life with great precision. You wish to offer yourself this in your relationships, your work, your opportunities and adventures, and most of all, in your internal universe.

Oh, and we get how cool the car is and what we also know is that when you begin truly living your life through these energies consistently, the car will be an easily attracted "side effect."

Breathing Your Own Breath~ In Union

Your world is in an ecstatic state of shifting from the energy of Separation into the energy of Union. Through breathing your own breath, you will find a most powerful tool right there within your being.

You might ask, "What is it to breathe my own breath, Mary? What does that mean? Haven't I always been breathing my own breath? Isn't it my breath that is within my physical, emotional, mental, and spiritual being? Isn't it the essence of me, this breath?"

Great questions!

In response, we offer to you this teaching: Yes, the breath that is moving through your body is indeed your breath. And yet, the only breath that was breathed by you and was truly and purely and wholly your own unique, free energy print—was the first one—the First Breath you inhaled and exhaled when you were born. After that First Breath, the energy of Separation that is so prevalent in the human experience, began to enter into the equation.

Over the years, we have been working with all of you who have moved with us, we have noticed to our puzzlement that many times, we would have to remind you to breathe. You are all so shallowly using this most wonderful, ease-filled, natural gift that each of you has—the breath. We are speaking of both the physical breath and the ethereal breath. Both bring you life-force energy in the physical and non-physical aspects of yourself.

We noticed that you are not breathing when you are challenged or when you are stressed and sometimes even when you are in a complete state of joy. You hold your breath as if trying to not let it be touched by something. A Separation energy, perhaps? And still, we urge you to breathe, breathe, breathe this life, this life force, this beautiful gift of breath. In the ethereal sense and the physical sense, breathe unafraid and with abandon, because the truth is that in breathing your own breath, you are free.

Oftentimes, when we point out this lack of breathing to somebody we are exchanging with, the person offers a little giggle and says, "Oh, you're right, Mary. I'm not breathing. I don't think I've been breathing for a very long time." Sometimes we have a little fun with telling you how surprised we are that you are not a little blue for lack of oxygen. Yet you are in the time now that each of you has agreed—every being on the planet has agreed—to be part of this movement from Separation into Union. That's what this "Breathing Your Own Breath" is about.

We know that it may sound interesting to have us say, "Breathe your own breath." You may wonder if it will actually cause even more Separation for everybody to be choosing to breathe his or her own breath individually, instead of moving to breathe one breath all together. We offer to you that the effect is actually the opposite. It is to breathe so clearly your own breath, your own unique expression—free, embraced, and celebrated—that you can actually be in and of any environment and in the Oneness without any need to keep yourself distant.

As you embrace and celebrate the unique and distinguishing qualities of yourself, you will easily and joyfully celebrate the uniqueness and the distinguishing qualities of every other being's inhale and exhale.

We invite you, in this moment, before we go any further, to just kind of wiggle your shoulders and settle into place. Let yourself be present. Let your mind relax. Open your Heart and invite your Soul to be full in its presence and your Spirit to be free in its effervescence and its ability to bring you lightness. To bring you the expansiveness that is your natural way. Relax the skin on your body a bit and the skin on your face and breathe a few breaths and arrive here into this moment. Truly arrive.

Let your spine be open and wide and allow the spinal fluid to let its golden liquid flow and trickle and move in peaceful elegance through your being. As it flows, moving with joy, it can also offer out porously to assist and love every part of you, physical and non-physical. Arrive.

Be of your Free Will. Always in Regard. Always loving. Always cherishing of yourself and everything in existence. Breathe and feel yourself home.

❦ ❦ ❦

As we mentioned before, we became very curious about this lack of breathing in your world. We began to wonder what is this not breathing the beautiful breath you have been given all about? We wondered at what point in a life does this practice of "held breath" begin. This inquiry took us all the way back to when you first came into your human expression, the time of your birth.

We found that this is true for every one of you. It does not matter what challenges may have been occurring or how you might have been impacted while you were in the womb. Even if there was a physical challenge upon your birth, for every one of you, your first breath was whole and pure and your own. You all get one.

When you come into the world and you draw that First Breath, you are in a state of absolute Arrival, Connectivity, Euphoria, Truth, All-knowing. In this state, you recognize your particles as having match points in all other particles. Your particles are significant in their uniqueness of expression of the "you" who came into a life of wholeness and came whole into a life of expression. Your expression. Your First Breath. The inhale is the knowing of your infinity, the knowing of your edgelessness and the thrill of arrival ... and exhale. Coming into your concreteness. Your roots beginning to grow. Your choosing of staying to have this experience. And breathe...

And then we noticed Second Breath ... very different. Second Breath on the inhale is you beginning to inhale your environment—all of the thoughts and beliefs and ideas in it, all of the influences, the tightnesses, the history. All that which is of Separation is also included. Not only included, but also very prevalent in your world for some time now. More years than your ability to comprehend can count. At Second Breath, you begin to breathe the environment: the Separation, the Fears, the Joys, the stories of those who are in it and the air itself of mass consciousness.

Second Breath is such a differing vibration because it holds Separation in it and First Breath only held Union: that knowing of all things and all connectivity. The absolute celebration of existence and life. Of self and of its sharing with everything else into Second Breath. Quite a different experience.

Every one of you who came in knew, "I will go and agree to play a role, to participate with Separation in this time of transformation, moving from Separation into Union. All as a whole, interactively." While you felt the distinct difference between First Breath and Second Breath, Union and Separation, you knew you had agreed.

What occurred in that moment is what we call "first tangle of Separation." The response system to that is: "I need to establish my existence so that I may stay because my energy feels different than this energy in which I just arrived. I need to acquire or participate or become weaved into or connected to assure my space in this existence. This is so I may continue to take another breath and another breath and another breath and to create that which I am in this world, in this energy of Separation."

That is where the movement of discontinuing breathing your own breath and instead breathing the breath of the situation, the energy, the environment, came in.

❦ ❦ ❦

We often recognize humans as fiction writers. Much of the time, you will interpret things, you will take one sight or sound or idea, then move it through your filters and write all kinds of stories. Many of these stories participate with Separation energy and have you trying to find your way, to hold your position, to assure that you exist. To assure you are received. That you are embraced and taken in by others.

Some of you have the experience of being joyfully received and embraced when you were born and some of you do not. We offer to you that much of the loving in your world is fearful loving. "I will protect you. I will keep you safe. I will teach you how to assimilate and how to be in this world so that you may fit in, or even so that you may stand out. However, stand out in a particular way that assures your continuation."

In these instances, not only are you breathing the breath of entanglement of assuring your own continued existence, so are those who are receiving you because they are breathing their entanglement of assuring their own existence. They want to also ensure your continuation of existence, to take you in. They may also be in their own wrestlings, that they have moved so far in Separation from themselves that perhaps they don't know how to demonstrate in any other fashion. This way of fearful loving leaves many feeling unreceived, unseen, and uncelebrated for being exactly who they are.

Breathing your own breath is about you stepping into knowing that you are whole and an edgeless resource for self. We absolutely offer you the knowing that you are received. You have always, always, always been whole and generously and admiringly held. You are received. You are seen. You are heard. You are embraced. You are cherished and celebrated. Whether there is a recognition of that or anything evidencing or recognizable about that in the physical reality of your world, it is so. It is your natural state to be received, to know you are of every particle of all existence and of the Oneness. You are a unique expression of the Oneness.

We often assist humans with understanding Union by looking to Nature. The reason we do that is because Nature has always breathed its own breath. Nature has always been of Union. It did not agree to participate with the energy of Separation. Never has. What we offer to you is that Nature is a constant and continuous state of connectivity.

We have great enjoyment of bringing you into your real-izing. When we speak about "real-izing," we are speaking about an activation to bring what is Real into expression, into wholeness. It is for you to "real-ize" yourself as the same Union as Nature.

Think about it this way. A particle of the atmosphere in Colorado knows about a particle of sand in the Sahara Desert. That the first cell of the first seed of a birth of a tree is aware of every molecule of water and of every sound that has ever moved through the ocean or through the tree on the breeze or through the unfolding of the grass as the critters move through it or come out from under its soil. That is actually the natural state of the human, too.

It is for you to know yourself, that inner nature so well, to have recognition that there is such a grand celebration and knowing of Union within you. Within every element of you. Within every movement of you and expression of you. To carry that out further into that connectivity, your sharing of that self as you choose, with all other life existence.

So breathe and relax and remember that you arrived into First Breath vibration whole and free and that, that is the center of your being.

The Ache we see in humans is about the closure, the confinement, of that First Breath. Of First Breath being put away to assure your own existence in the midst of Separation energy. Of its being confined or condensed, its not being a full-open, absolute celebration of your arrival and your received and your receiving of you as a life, and you of a life, and you as a unique expression of all life.

As Nature breathes in Union, you have that within you, too. As you begin to breathe your own breath, that Ache will yield to the knowing that you are whole and free. There is no need for the Ache any longer. Your full connectivity with the divinity of that moving flow of your wholeness is there.

❧ ❧ ❧

When we speak about the practice of breathing your own breath, we're not talking about just in quiet spaces or in moments where you can sneak away and string together a couple of breaths for yourself. We are speaking about every breath you draw and exhale for the rest of your life in every environment and every situation. That full awakening and arrival that, "I am breathing my own breath. I am not tangled with that which has tangles in it any longer. With that which holds Separation. I am waking into my full Union expression. I choose this Union. I choose this Arrived. I choose this Received. I choose to know this in every moment that I breathe and I breathe them all."

We hear many say, "Mary, it feels easy to do this when I am with certain people who feel like they understand me or that I understand them, in a space where I am inspired and, of course, in Nature."

Many of you have at least one element or space in Nature in which you can feel your rhythm. To completely give yourself its wholeness and to allow the wholeness of Nature to be found within you. Yet we are speaking about doing it in any environment, so that it doesn't matter what is occurring in your world. That you are showing up as this whole-being expression with the awakened First Breath. The vibration that is shifting so powerfully.

It is time for you to know that you are the grandest knower of you. There is no other physical or non-physical that can really breathe the way you would breathe in most exquisiteness with self. Yet, we know that because of all of the Separation, perhaps a guided tour to find your way there is helpful. We are more than of great gratitude to be able to assist you with this.

Perhaps look to the imagery of sea grass in Nature. If you consider the sea grass for a moment, and maybe for those of you who wish to, allow the feeling, the sensation of you becoming sea grass and kind of just moving on the waves of the current. Sea grasses, we have noticed, move and bump into each other and gather many things and coat themselves and divest themselves and move on the current.

It isn't about the sea grass waking every day and saying, "I will choose what is in my current," or "I will choose what I participate with in my current." It is that the sea grass knows it is of Union and there will be many things in the current. Sometimes the current will even hold complete stillness. It is extraordinary to be in the midst of all that is in the current. All the breaths that are breathing in the current. All the movement that is there. Knowing that "I am this sea grass and I am moving as I choose to. Sharing and perhaps as I bump into the sea grass next to me or I shake my root a little bit to send a signal a thousand miles across the ocean floor to shimmy into another sea grass blade. To share with it something that it wishes to pull up from this root system. And yet, we don't tangle."

When we offer this concept, we invite to you recognize that it is not about non-participation with one another. It is about absolute participation with one another without losing the self or restricting the self or being confined or being afraid of one another.

It is getting so clear and so whole on this First Breath and breathing your own breath within the self that you no longer fear you. Any part of you. Because you are coming into the connectivity of Union energy of every other part's role. You are knowing that life is being played out and signaled divinely and perfectly to bring you the most extraordinary wholeness of life expression.

So be the sea grass as you waken into your day and know that there are many things that will move in the current of your life. Some that you enjoy and some that you will let pass by. No longer getting into the tangle or attempting to put up shields or fend yourself off from because you know all that is in the current can simply move through and you are this free, beautiful, divine being of expression.

We are talking about absolute truth and connectivity and spark of life experienced and unexperienced. Thriving. As you cease to be afraid of yourself, you will cease to be afraid of anything outside of you. As you allow yourself to recognize and embrace and celebrate and adore this self that you are, then you will thrive and you exude that thriving. You won't be responsible for anybody outside of you. You will care for them beautifully without False Fear. And allow yourself to be exchanged with in the same way.

"I am free and I am breathing my own breath, beside you breathing your own breath, beside you breathing your own breath, and so on."

We are not only speaking of the humans; we are speaking of all life expression. "I breathe my own breath." Awaken into it. Arrive into this expression that is me to release the Ache of the disconnect of Separation. To feel that wholeness of that true and pure and whole breath, your breath, moving through you, getting you a bit high because it is offering oxygen into spaces that have been closed or unknown to you for so long. And, very importantly, it is opening the lift energy of Truth. Opening, arriving, received, received, received. Always in every moment.

"I belong in this existence that I am and in this existence that is. I get to be free in my expression inside of me and outside of me without fear." That is the choosing of breathing your own breath. "I invite, I instigate, I inspire all else to breathe its own breath in that same freedom so that we may all be unbound from the tangles of Separation and return to the truth of Union."

You are so ready to breathe this first breath. To awaken and unchain yourself from the separations and the bindings and the guards at the door and the pain prisons and the fracture points and all of those things that have been built from the catalyst of that first tangle of Separation.

You may have forgotten that First Breath was absolute and automatic in the most extraordinary way. Of course, you exist and are real. Not because of anything outside of you that evidences that. Instead, because you are and it is so. You get to breathe this infinite breath of Union and Wholeness and Arrival and Received. You choose to move in that pulse, as that current around you can hold anything in it, and you can still know you are

Well. You can release yourself from the tangles and the Tightness and the Discord and the Disregard and the Unreceived. Those can still be in the current and yet your vibration won't match those tangles any longer.

As you breathe this opening, this awakening, you will live this expression of your First Breath—this awakening of your own breath—and grow it and grow it and grow it in the intelligence that your being tells you is the best rate and the best way for it to occur.

Trust your natural intellect. By "intellect," we are not speaking about how you can analyze or associate or prove anything. We are talking about an intellect that is so divine and so natural and so real and whole within you, that as you open into it, there is an "Ahhhhhhh, yes, of course I never felt like I "fit" or that I knew how to place myself, because I didn't match those energies, and yet there are energies that I do match and that I am. As I awaken into them, my energy can be anywhere and know that it is matched. That my energy has its own wholeness wherever it is because it has all of me with it and I am with it in my wholeness."

You are the sea grass so you are not fearful to allow anything to be in connectivity with your existence. However, you do get to choose what you participate with freely. Not because you are guarding yourself or are separate from it. Instead because it is just about choosing, and exchanging your curiosity and experimenting and learning, discovering, expanding, and being whole in your union. In your truth. In your celebration of self and all that is.

We are very excited about being with you now, during this transition from Separation to Union. It is our great honor to bring you this tool of breathing your own breath and to recognize your arriving untangled, this beautiful gift you are in every moment.

(If you are interested in learning more about this concept and receiving the attunements to take you fully into the vibration of your First Breath and to open you to breathing your own breath every day for the rest of your life, check out our website, www.themarygroup.com for details on offerings of this process.)

Creating the Dream of You

When you live from the energy of the aspects associated with your dream, your vision... whatever it may be—Freedom, Confidence, Ease, Excitement—you begin to experience changes in everything in your life.

You have to be it on the inside to attract it, create it, and recognize it on the outside.

That's just the way it is. We are aware that this concept is most perplexing to many people. You are so used to attempting to create from the outside in, like this: "If I had a really great car or relationship or job or opportunity, then I would be Happy." In truth, the way it works is that you choose to be Happy and the things that match the frequency of Happiness will begin to show up. Actually, they may have been there the whole time; you just weren't able to see or feel them because you were not a match to them while you were choosing Unhappiness as one of your front-running aspects.

You see, everything in all existence is vibration, including you. When you are vibrating something such as Happiness, you emit a frequency that can be seen and felt by other life expressions in the world that are also vibrating with Happiness, at least to some degree. If you are not vibrating with Happiness, these things, people, and opportunities cannot even see you.

This is true even if this vibration is being practiced within a person or a place you encounter on a regular basis. That is why sometimes, one person can walk by a park every day on the way to work and hardly notice it, while a workmate might walk by the same park and be captivated by its open invitation to breathe in life and notice the simplicities of beauty that feed the workmate's internal Happiness. It doesn't mean one of them is doing it right and the other is doing it wrong. It just means that they are each showing up very differently for the exchange and therefore having a very different experience. The park naturally vibrates in a Happiness frequency. The person passing by who is also emitting this frequency identifies with it and feels its invitation and welcome, while the person who is not emitting this frequency simply passes it by without incident or exchange.

You may say to us, "That all sounds good, Mary. Can you tell me how to feel my Happiness when it has been so long since I have visited with it that I don't even know what it feels like anymore."

We may first ask you if you are, in full truth, willing to change your current story about your lack of Happiness. If you indeed found your way to say and mean "yes," then we may suggest you invite Happiness to rise up in you for a visit. Let it know what kind of relationship you intend and are activating as you move forward in your life.

Then we would encourage you to invest your time, love, and attention in this newly forming relationship. Really lean into it, give yourself to it fully, let it have you, know you, share itself with you. Look to see Happiness in everything you do, experience, and feel. Trace its reflection into the intricacies of your heart and soul and let your mind know what you are up to, so it knows how to respond in your thoughts and memory retrievals.

Open yourself completely to the vibration of your Happiness. Pulse with it in all that you do. Release yourself from any practiced belief that you are separate from Happiness in any way. Breathe it in and out, building on it one particle at a time, until it becomes the most natural thing in your world. Be one with it. You just have to give yourself permission and change your story.

🌱 🌱 🌱

We have a long-time friend known to us in physical interaction almost as long as we have been with Don and Jacque. We have had the great joy and pleasure to interact with her often as she explores and creates her chosen life. When we met her, she was a single woman with a job that somewhat suited but did not excite her, a life that she was appreciative of, with friends and family, and felt OK enough. However, her life was not completely fulfilling, and she had a clearly expressed desire to find her "soulmate." She came to us eager and curious and open to soak in new information and understanding that would fill her and take her to new places of creation in her experience of self. And so began our journey together.

She is a rather remarkable and precise person who knew what she wanted and somehow was also often willing to settle for "good enough." This was the paradox. She had high ideals matched to her true and authentic self, and yet she had practices in thought and choosing that accommodated results that were less than fulfilling. While she was a naturally positive person, she often felt frustrated, defensive, and uninspired, longing for something more.

Over the time we worked together, she moved to identify and shift internal confusions, fracture points, her coat of armor, her inability to fully receive, and the outside-in messages that didn't match her sensibilities. She had designed herself through these anyway, with senses of Loss, Self-bullying, and Judgment, with an overall feeling of Not-Good-Enough. During this time, she tried on a few relationships that weren't a match and fizzled out, a new career idea or two that never found their fruition, and a couple rearrangements of the circumstances in her life that brought some relief, but not the complete freedom she desired.

So now, the blanket was off. She had exposed herself to the truth of herself and could no longer pretend that everything was OK as it was. It was at this point that she began to use Frustration as a catalyst for change, instead of a place to find a way to be comfortable living in. She began to identify herself through the truth that she was Whole and Worthy and Deserving (not entitled) of the life she dreamed for herself. A life filled with a reflection of the Generosity and Love that she is. A life that boldly lived itself through Truth, Curiosity, and Discovery and took herself into account in every choice she made. A life that no longer settled for "good enough" and instead, created and held tightly to her own ideals of what she chose to create on the inside and the outside of her. A life that felt Free with Ease and partnership that matched her belief in herself and in a fulfilling life.

She had come home to and embraced her authentic self, who had always believed in her and now had opportunity to pulse her Truth of Self-Conviction through all of her thoughts, beliefs, practices, and creations with great love.

These internal shifts caused her to draw to herself deeper connections with friends she had always felt love for, but had been holding outside the coat of armor she wore. She also released old patterns in how she showed up for all of her relationships that did not garner the respect and appreciation for her and for which she now felt available. She drew resources to herself that are alleviating her financial concerns and are opening the doors for further career exploration.

In addition, she attracted her perfect mate, a point-for-point match to her desire in partnership. She is now flourishing in living herself in "More-Than-Enough."

There were moments in this process that she threw a fit over there being one more layer, one more adjustment, one more disconnect, calling to her to move it. Now she is very clear that nothing on the outside of her was shiftable until she shifted the inside and was happy to have left no stone unturned in the claiming of her life and her dream of herself.

The Judgment Trap

Judgment is one of the first aspects that humans encounter upon entry into your world. This is due to the fact that in many cultures, it is pervasively practiced by society as a whole. The aspect of Judgment itself is not detrimental to a life of known Well-being. However, when you mix Judgment with False Fear, it is likely to cause a choosing of Separation between you and what is being judged, whether it be inside or outside of you.

To encourage people to withdraw their participation in the continuation of this separating activity, we often offer the practice of "Match, Not a Match" as a way of walking through life without the adverse impact of Judgment. Using "Match, Not a Match" is also a way of recognizing where you are vibrating from day to day. Imagine showing up for your moments observing, experiencing, and choosing, instead of judging and pushing against.

If you come into exchange with somebody who does not match your sensibilities, values, or personality, you don't need to spend one ounce of your precious energy making that person wrong or attempting to convince that person to be different, or rejecting that person. You simply note, "Not a Match" and allow the person and you to be yourselves, respectively. Then move on with your day and your chosen state of existence. This really is possible, even if the person is somebody you encounter every day or maybe even live with. It is just a matter of discontinuing the battle—internally and externally.

"But that's taking the path of least resistance," you might say. This does not mean you will lie down and "take it." Quite the opposite, actually. It means you are making a choice to stay powerfully in your known Well-being, without the fear that somebody or something outside of you can change that without your permission.

It is key, however, to stop giving others permission to influence you more powerfully than you influence yourself. Stop abandoning yourself in favor of listening to and believing in people and things outside of you more powerfully than you believe in and listen to yourself. Instead, be available to receive what is being offered and then decide if it is for you or not. Match, or Not a Match.

On the other hand, you sometimes come into contact with others who really spark your interest, raise your curiosity, and tingle your allure antenna. You lean in closer to draw more from your connection with them. Perhaps their particular brand of intellect or heart-centered energy gets you excited and willing to open up for more. That is a Match. "More of that for me, please.

I feel myself here." Know that the Match you are finding in these instances reflects the places inside of you saying, "YES!" Living this "yes" is not dependent on anybody outside of you to have this ongoing relationship with yourself. Of course, it is fun to have company along the way. Enjoy.

❦ ❦ ❦

Audience: So, Mary, I am wondering if you could help me get everybody in my life and maybe even everybody in the world to just see it my way and do things the way I would like them to?

Mary: HA! Is that really what you would want? (*audience laughs*)

Audience: Seems to me it would make things a whole lot more enjoyable.

Mary: For whom?

Audience: For me.

Mary: Would it really? What would there be to stimulate you?

Audience: I am a pretty clever guy. I could come up with ideas for others to follow along with.

Mary: We believe you would get very bored very quickly. And, also very frustrated and exhausted because now you have all of these people to run and coordinate.

Audience: Ok. I know I am exaggerating but really, I am exhausted now from all of the careless, idiotic, and disappointing behavior in others. And not just people. Systems, too. It feels like the world is going to hell in a hand basket and I am just supposed to sit by and say, "Oh well…" and let it go on?

Mary: Well, in a sense, we suppose we are suggesting that. Do you know that right now, in this room full of a wide variety of beautiful, loving, and caring people, there are those who are judging you as negative about how you are judging the world as a lost cause? And there are those who are nodding their heads yes and judging you as right on the mark as they are finding agreement with you within themselves.

So in this room, there are those who agree and those who don't and those who are neutral. And by the way, some of those who don't agree are the ones who you came with. (*Person asking the questions gives an intentional evil eye to his friends and audience laughs*)

Of course, as we look at you, we can clearly recognize that you are a caring and loving being who is temporarily experiencing some situations that have brought you to some dismal and negative feelings about your purpose in life or the purpose of life in general. Because you are operating from this vibration, what you are noticing in the people and situations around you are the dismal and negative aspects of them.

When you release yourself from the burdens of your situations and give yourself permission to once again recognize yourself as a self, separate from the situations you are weighted by, you will once again begin to fill with the love and belief that you are. You will begin to notice those things in others and situations instead.

Audience: So you are saying that I am seeing and experiencing the world through the burden of my current situations? And that is why I am feeling frustrated with others?

Mary: Yes, that is exactly what we are saying. We see it happen all the time. And because you are feeling out of control for your own experience, you are living the energy of the situation instead of the energy of the self, and you feel a need to push back and control your environment to regain your inner control.

Audience: Wow! So I don't want to control others, I want to control myself.

Mary: Yes. Just take this room of people and consider you taking on the responsibility for what they think and believe in, how they act or respond to you and all in the world in every moment of every day, what choices they make and what aspects from within them they live through in what moments...

Audience: OK, OK...that is not what I want.

Mary: What is it that you really want?

Audience: To not feel so frustrated and disappointed with situations and others so often.

Mary: Ah, so now we are talking about something that is truly within your control—how you feel, how you choose, how you create.

Audience: Yes, that sounds interesting.

Mary: Can you already feel a difference in your energy when you consider how you might simply choose differently to suit yourself in your situations? In other words, to decide how you will or will not participate in your situations, in comparison to what it would take to get others to choose differently to suit you in those situations.

Audience: (*smiling*) Yes, I can feel that. I am not sure how to get there, though.

Mary: Well, that is where we can come in handy for you. (*audience laughs.*)

Audience: Good.

Mary: Your world is designed to have great variety and many hues of contrast. None of you would remain entertained enough to stay if it did not. How you move with that contrast and whether you create more opportunity or less opportunity for yourself as a result of it is up to you.

You were never meant to agree with or participate with every other thought, belief, or action on the planet, but you were meant to acquire whatever might be beneficial to you from them. When there is nothing beneficial for you about them, then it is simply Not a Match for you and you can pass it by. This might mean that some parts of a situation are Not a Match and some parts are, or it might mean that it is a full Match or Not a Match at all.

Audience: OK.

Mary: Would you really wish to live in a world that just had one way, even it was *your* way?

Audience: No, I suppose I wouldn't. I would like to have more experiences where it felt like people were on board for my ideas or way of being, though.

Mary: Good. That is a far cry from being the oppressive ruler of the world who required all obey you and never have a differing thought or do things that you would not choose to do. (*smiles*)

Audience: Yes, that is true.

Mary: We are truth-tellers.

Audience: Yes, I can feel that.

Mary: So, as you go forward from this moment, are you willing to remember that you are a self living in a world with great variety to choose from and as a self, you are also a chooser and so is everybody else? Are you willing to remember that you are all free to choose how you show up in your life, what matches for you in other people or situations, and what doesn't.

Are you willing to move always to care for and take care of yourself, while caring for others and not taking care of them? Because truly, even though your way might feel like the right way to you, it might not feel like the right way to them, just as theirs does not feel like a Match for you.

Audience: I am going to give it a shot.

Mary: Good. Thank you. Your choice to stop separating yourself from your life by judging others and to start living through your own choices, what is important to you, and matches you instead, offers much to you and to the world.

What's Up with My Intimate Relationships?

When moving in an intimate relationship with a partner, it might be enlightening for you to be aware that there are three distinct existences of consciousness within a relationship. These three conscious existences are: You, the Relationship Itself, and your Partner.

While it is a common practice to identify the strength of your relationship through what your partner is doing or not doing, to have a fulfilling relationship that is understood and enjoyed by you, it is important that you put first things first—in this case, that means *you*. Now, we don't mean that you need to make yourself first in the relationship. Actually, it is more satisfying to give equal value to all three existences—if you desire a balanced and harmonious relationship, that is.

What we are saying is that when moving through the multitude of nuances and occurrences in an intimate relationship, the most rewarding and fortuitous outcome of the journey always begins within, with the relationship you have with yourself. From there, it is about your relationship to the consciousness of the relationship itself—this "life form" that the two of you have created as a result of choosing to navigate life together in partnership. Then finally, it is about your relationship to your partner.

We often witness this as the opposite way of how many of you move in relationship. For instance, when something is not feeling good in your relationship, you tend to look at the other person and consider what it is that person needs to be doing differently to make the relationship stronger or more fulfilling for you. Come on, just admit it. You have done this at least once in your experience.

When you find yourself wishing somebody or something outside of you would be different so you could be more Comfortable, more Fulfilled, or more Satisfied, that is the perfect time to examine your relationship with yourself. For instance, if you are feeling abandoned in a relationship, you may want to examine how you may be abandoning yourself in association with the relationship. Or if you are feeling mistrusting of the other person in the relationship, you may want to look at your Mistrust of yourself to honor yourself when it comes to your choices around the relationship.

Remember, if it is going on in your world outside of you, then it is going on inside of you to some degree. Many people lose themselves or, perhaps more accurately stated, give themselves away to relationships and then blame the other person for taking advantage of them. You cannot be taken advantage of in this way without your permission. It may have occurred little by little, kind of sneaking up on you, never feeling like you were giving too much away at one time, and then it all adds up and you feel lost to yourself.

Instead of blaming the other person and therefore moving in the belief that another could actually have this kind of power over you, tell yourself the truth. "I did it again. I gave myself away to this partner. I molded myself to what I thought I needed to be to continue to match to that person, and now I am unfulfilled. I did that. It is just the truth."

Then grab yourself by the scruff of the neck and pull yourself into your warmest, welcome-back embrace. Release the Blame and release yourself as Victim. From there you can make some very clear and loving choices about yourself and your relationship, because now you are there, in your own body, with your own Self-awareness, to make positively impacting choices.

On the flip side, when your relationship is Strong, joyful, and oh so yummy, it is also good to begin at home, inside of you, and offer yourself recognition of what you have done to influence this outcome through your relationship with yourself, your relationship with the relationship itself, and your relationship with your partner. Then you can also look at and recognize what your partner has offered to himself or herself, the relationship itself, and to you—and relish in the gratitude for the Grace of Real Loving.

The consciousness of your relationship is constantly impacted and developed as a result of what each of you is doing in relationship with yourselves and with one another. When both of you are activated and engaged in this process, the Blaming, Fear, and Separation stops and the true Union within and between you can thrive.

These principles do not apply just to your intimate relationships. They are true for your family relationships, friendships, work relationships, and even your incidental relationships that happen in passing, such as the one with the clerk at the store, or the person standing in front of or behind you in line. The moment two people interact for the first time, whether words are part of the experience or not, the consciousness of a relationship comes into existence. Isn't that kind of fun, to know that you are birthing conscious existence all the time?

The more you are willing to explore and reach into yourself for the truth and discovery of what you create into experience within the relationships—or how you are moving in response to the experiences that develop and give form to the relationships— the bigger sense of Satisfaction and Flow you will feel in yourself, in the relationship and with the other person.

On the other hand, the less you are willing to identify and own yourself and make choices based on your relationship with yourself as a key factor to what is moving or not moving for you in yourself and in the relationship, the less fulfilling it will be.

Remember, you are always the one you are seeking in relationship. Let yourself be Found, Enjoyed, and lovingly Honored in connection with the relationship and the other person involved, instead of attempting to have this result be because of that person.

We have had the pleasure of ongoing conversations with a woman who has been involved in her intimate relationship for a number of years. While mostly happily satisfied with the course and experience of this relationship, she has come to us wrapped in utter frustration with the fact that most every time she addresses a conflict or issue between her and her husband, she is always, in the end, identified as "the one with the problem."

She expressed that this infuriates her and leaves her with no sense of feeling seen or heard by her husband. She stated that it makes her feel like she doesn't even know how to address things with him that will cause him to see and own what he is doing that doesn't feel good to her because of his apparent mastery in always turning it around and making it about her. This is not making it about her in a way that feels embraced; instead, it leaves her reeling in wonder as to how this issue once again became hers.

She went on lamenting for a bit about the dissatisfaction of these conversations to make him have recognition of how his behavior and choices affect her and to take responsibility for that and agree to change it. She asked us how she can get him to stop being so exasperating in his unwillingness to ever just once apologize. She also wanted to know how to respond to his constant ability to go on to criticize her for what she does to confine or restrict his "just being him."

We let her go on for as long as she needed to and when she came to a resting place, we began to ask her questions about her and her relationship with herself. We asked her to consider how she relates to herself. Is she consistently Kind and Loving to herself? She said probably not as often as she would like to be.

We asked her if she made herself an important person in her life, somebody to be Valued and Celebrated by herself. She just grinned and said she mostly tries to make sure that others feel that way, and that her conversations with herself were more Self-critical and Questioning. This bothered her because she would like to feel like she has great Value, but recognizes that this has been something she has always either had to "fight for" or has just worked to press herself into the wallpaper so as not to be seen for being Less-Than-Enough to satisfy or please another.

We asked her why she felt frustrated about the things she brought up to her husband and what type of things she felt important to address with her husband. She got a little teary and said that a scream would just start to form in her—a scream to be Noticed and Recognized through words or action. She said she wasn't really even looking for much, just something. Or, at least, for him to stop making comments about how he could live without her, that he didn't need her or anybody else to be OK. He could be fine on his own if he had to be. Her tears increased now and she said that she just wanted to feel Important to him, instead of dispensable. She wanted to be Desired, Sought, and Received by him.

All the while she was talking and crying, we could see a light going on inside her and she said, "Oh, my God. Here I am again. This time I am talking to you and I am being shown that my problem or my pain is not about him, it is about me." Her defenses began to rise and she considered pulling away from us and using some quite colorful words to tell us what she thought about that.

Then we said, "What he is or isn't doing that hasn't been feeling good for you is not about you; it is about him. It certainly impacts you and still it is about him. What you are here to discover today is not about him, it is about you. About you Seeing, Caring for, and Choosing you by being here to have this conversation. Being here to cause a shift in yourself so you can feel Good and know your Value." She began to relax and breathe and release her defenses.

We went on to share with her that the confusion she was experiencing and acting on was that what needed to change was her husband's behaviors and ownership of his "failures" in their relationship. So we spoke with her about considering making some changes in her relationship with herself. We moved with her to find the sources or practices of her Disconnect from herself that left her feeling the need for outside-in confirmation of her value in relationships. We helped her to recognize that doing this was the only real way to change things for her.

If she was willing to heal the fractures in the relationship she had with herself, she would shift her energy and her concept of herself. That would bring to her the sense of Calm and Peace she was looking for.

From that connected place of self, we then encouraged her to look at the relationship itself and who she was in relationship to it. How does she show up for it? How does she feed or starve it? What does she contribute to herself and to her husband through it? How does she care for it? This conversation took a bit of time as we had to keep pulling her back to just considering herself in relationship to herself and the relationship itself, instead of side-tracking to what and how he was doing or not doing things.

She quickly got good at catching herself and admitted that the lure to make this about him at this point was difficult to deny. She called up her rather wonderful Humor to help her in the process so she would not fall back into Judging herself for her getting off track. Several times throughout this part of the conversation, we asked her to consider if it was of interest for her to continue engaging with the entity of the relationship. She expressed Happiness that it was indeed something she felt deeply and Joyfully Committed to continuing to be involved with.

With that identified, we went onto him. Who was she in relationship to him? She got very excited as she spoke of feeling a big shift in her. She felt that she was seeing him through new eyes. He was no longer somebody she identified herself through. She now recognized herself clearly as a free-standing self, not dependent on his Appreciation to know and feel her Wholeness. She knew she had more work to do to solidify this feeling, but was very clearly understanding that she had been trying to find herself through him and that she was never going to find herself there.

She recognized that she had to show up as a Whole in the relationship and so did he. Both of them showing up Whole would allow for them to *care for* instead of attempting to *take care of* or *be taken care of* by one another. This would allow the opening for true Cherishing of what they added to each other, instead of feeling like they had to guard against what could or is being taken away.

From this place of vibration, she would not attract his jabs so often and when they did come, it would be an opportunity for her to choose herself through Love and decline them. She could also stop throwing at him her unattainable demands and requirements of how and who he was in any given moment to make her feel whole.

Later, we heard from her husband, who wanted to come speak with us to gain the same understanding for himself, so they could both have this knowing and move forward in Union.

Love, Safety, and Value

There are three spaces within the human that must be in some sense of balance for you to feel your complete flow: the Knowing of Love; the Feeling of Safety, and the Experience of Being Valued.

The confusion for humans comes in when they make this balance dependent on what is offered from people and situations outside of them. This is where many humans unwittingly turn their lives over to others and attempt to make the others responsible for their own Happiness, Self-Worth, Peacefulness, Fulfillment, and so on.

Then, when those people or situations outside you "fail" in this task, you become Resentful and Dissatisfied with them. You begin judging them wrong and no longer a Match to you. To a degree, you are correct about the Match no longer fitting. However, many times it is not because they have changed; it is because when you invited people or situations into your life, you were actually there in your own skin—and now you are not. You have changed in a direction away from yourself, no longer matching who you were before you made yourself and your satisfaction with life dependent on something or someone outside of you.

For instance, perhaps you have decided that getting a certain job or certain type of job, would allow you to feel seen and valued for your talents and skills and therefore Loved, Appreciated, and Safe as well. So you embark on a path to seek out this job and make it your own and you are successful in acquiring what feels like the perfect job to accomplish this endeavor. It is all very exciting...for a little while. Then, after a couple of weeks or even months, you slowly become a bit Disenchanted or Disgruntled. You begin to think and speak badly of the company or your boss or your co-workers. You don't feel Seen or Appreciated by them for your great ideas or skills. You eventually find yourself as much or more dissatisfied with this job as you did the last one that felt Unfulfilling and left you Drained instead of Thriving.

This is all because of the "outside-in" point of creation you began with: the "maybe if I get this job, or this thing, or this relationship...then I will feel Loved, Safe, and Valued." This will happen over and over again in every arena of your life until you begin and continue to understand that your life and your happiness—your feeling your balance in these three areas—are an "inside-out" job.

It is all about you. It is really not up to the job or the person or the thing outside of you to bring you your Love, Safety, and Value. It is up to you to bring your Love, Safety, and Value to yourself and then to them. In doing so, you don't get lost and you are able to garner and be available to receive the matching Recognition of you that you have for yourself.

The "take responsibility for my life, please" happens the other way around as well. We are speaking of the crushing, burdened feeling of having somebody whom you have grown to care about or become intricately connected to in some fashion, attempt to make you responsible for him or her. When you first met, you may have admired this person for standing in his or her own skin and heart and mind. And then, one day, you can't seem to find that person there anymore. There is not much recognizable about that person in association with the person you first met, or thought you met. You feel that person attempting to control or change you to meet the neediness that was born of the Abandonment of Self.

What has happened is that the person has forgotten that he or she, from the inside out, has full access to the knowing of Love, the experience of being Safe with the self, and the experience of Valuing the self. Because of this Forgetting, the person is no longer a match to you.

We watch this pattern repeated time and time again in every type of relationship ever invented or experienced. So what would happen if each and every one of you embraced the power of owning your own balance in these arenas? The answer: The burden of Obligation in relationship would fall away and the edgelessness of True, Ecstatic Connection to self and others would be known and experienced by all. Go ahead, start a revolution and let it begin with you.

❦ ❦ ❦

We will tell you at story about a dear friend who moved through this experience. This woman has a rather close-knit group of friends with whom she has nurtured beautiful and loving relationships and has trusted a great deal over a number of years. One day, as they were all gathered together, she decided that she would confide in them a self-doubt she was experiencing. She was tenuous in doing this because she believed sharing it had great potential to render her very Vulnerable. Even though she had faith in her relationships with these friends, she still wrestled with finding Comfort in her own vulnerability.

As she moved forward in sharing her Self-doubt with them, she was met with a variety of responses, including Surprise, Questioning, and some degree of Dismay. She could feel herself begin to close up and move into great Defense and Self-Protection mode as she experienced a feeling of Betrayal and Mistrust begin to rise in her as a result of their responses.

She did not feel very safe in a space where she had expected and required safety. Her belief in their Love and Embrace of her value seemed very distant to her. Her mind and heart were racing to find something to hold onto, when she had a clear Recognition that it was not their responses that were throwing her out of balance; it was her willingness to make her internal balance of Love, Safety, and Value dependent on their responses that was truly threatening her. In that instant, she called herself back into her body, remembered her own constant state of Well-being and without Fear, truly opened herself to her friends and all their reactions.

With the decision to own and believe in herself, the energy in the room and in her friends shifted and calmed. They began responding to her Confidence and Allowing, instead of Reacting, to the previous jumbled energy she had been carrying. This had been activated by her predetermined belief that she would be Vulnerable and Challenged when she exposed her Self-doubt.

Once she felt Loved, Safe, and Valued by herself, she no longer felt Unloved, Unsafe, or lacking Value with the others. Her choice to remember that she was Well and release her friends from the obligation to respond in the "right" way so she could feel Loved, Safe, and Valued, freed them all to have a real moment and continuing relationship of Connection.

Excuses, Defensiveness, Blaming, and Justification

We would like to offer you the rather enormous challenge of creating your life in the absence of excuses, defenses, blaming, and justification. Just think of how delicious it would be to live from your center, deliberately owning every moment of your life, feeling the exhilarating and powerful sense of Embracing and Belonging to you, without ever giving yourself away to the temptation of Disappearing, Hiding, or Dodging through excuses, defending, blaming, or justifying yourself.

Success with embracing and implementing this new way of living your life hinges on your real and committed acceptance of the notion that you are the Creator of your life. Your recognition that the way you think, choose, and cause yourself forward into the moments of your unfolding life is what creates your Self-identifying and your outcomes. Your freedom in the internal separations and fractures that living excuses, blaming, defenses, and justifications is also contingent on your willingness to come completely *OUT OF HIDING*. Yes, you, hiding. Hiding from everything you can imagine, including yourself.

It is inevitable that the majority of humans will offer this practice of Hiding in their lives to some degree, because almost right out of the starting gate of life, as soon as you have the ability to communicate and comprehend, Judgment begins. You respond by Shrinking (Hiding); Curbing yourself in some way to please another (Hiding); acting as if you didn't do what others say you did, when the truth is, you did (Hiding); causing the focus to go to another so it is off of you (Hiding)...you get the picture.

The interesting thing is, you don't only hide in response to negative Judgment. Sometimes you do it to deflect positive judgment so that you do not become set apart from others, become "different"...a "stand-out"...a "giant." Or maybe you duck the positive Judgment because it comes with a sense of responsibility to always get great grades and rise in achievement above the rest, to always have extraordinary insight and the right answer for people, to always hit the ball faster, farther, and harder than anybody else...you get the picture.

As far as the negative Judgments that encourage people to retreat or hide in some measure or another, let's try these commonly utilized "correcting directives" on for size. They are usually for children and encourage Hiding early on. They are frequently utilized in your world. See if any of them are familiar to you:

- ❦ Don't slouch.
- ❦ Don't belch.
- ❦ Don't laugh too loud.
- ❦ Don't wiggle so much.
- ❦ Don't boast.
- ❦ Don't argue.
- ❦ Don't beg.
- ❦ Don't be so big for your britches.
- ❦ Get your head out of the clouds.
- ❦ Quit dreaming.
- ❦ Your energy is too big in the room.
- ❦ Stop eating like a pig.
- ❦ Sit up straight.
- ❦ Get your face out of those books and go play.
- ❦ Settle down.
- ❦ Don't be such a goof-off.
- ❦ Be more serious about your future.
- ❦ Don't be inappropriate.
- ❦ Quit being a show off...

And these are just the tip of the iceberg! We find it a wonder that any of you are able to maintain even a speck of your individuality and genuine, authentic character at all under such a barrage of "corrections."

We haven't even addressed the Holding Spaces within you where you store all of the "should" and "should nots" yet! No wonder you are Hiding. No wonder you are filled with stagnant, closed, and guarded spaces. No wonder you hide and use excuses, blaming, defenses, and justifications voraciously, with great skill and a ready stance. So much so that most of your responses are on "automatic."

We are knowing that even as you read these words, you have no idea how steeped you truly may be in these practices. And still, we invite you to consider living without them or at least without as many of them as you have been.

Exquisite, really, the life lived without excuses, defenses, blaming, and justifications to such an exaggerated degree as we witness them being used in your world. For the purposes of having any modicum of success in this endeavor, if you choose to take it on, we suggest you only tackle one at a time. Or just stick the tip of your toe into all four to begin with. Trying to dive in and conquer these well-ingrained routines all at once will likely bring you to more frustration and futile realization than you are truly wanting to bargain with in any given moment.

So then, together, let's explore them each individually, shall we?

❧ ❧ ❧

Living Your Life Without Excuses

To grasp this idea, it will be important that you understand what constitutes an excuse. Excuses come in more

forms than you might suspect. Some of the most prevalent identifying markers of excuses are easily detected in
human thinking and in words that include "because,"
"if," "but," and so on. Most usually, these words chain
themselves together with other words that identify something outside of you or "beyond your control." An excuse is the reason for why you did not choose to do
something or indeed why you did choose to do something that you now would think twice about doing or
just plain ole don't want to admit to. For example, "I
would eat better if I had or if there were..."

Perhaps "but" is your preferred deferral. "I really
want to be a better manifester, dreamer, worker, spouse,
but ..."

For the purpose of experiment, we would like to offer
you a practice to take into your tomorrow. Begin your
day with a small, blank notepad. It is important that you
pick it up at first awareness when you awaken. The reason to have the notepad available that quickly is because
many of you begin with your practices of excuses before
you even roll out of bed.

Throughout the day, armed with Truth and Humor,
carry the pad with you and note each time you notice
any thought, rising belief that you are toying with, or
words you speak that include the vibration of excuse
energy. Even if you are not sure it is an excuse, write it
down. Some of you may need to write very small, even
tiny, or carry a very large pad. Ha!

Some of you may not use much of your pad at all because you will be busy making excuses as to why certain thoughts and words don't need to be considered an excuse and written down. Or, you may have an excuse for why carrying a pad will not work for you

The idea of this exercise is just to notice when you are "squirming," making excuses to any degree. This also includes adjusting your language, modifying a story of a happening in any way to deflect, cover, soften, or perhaps enhance your role in it. It can also be altering your presentation of self in any way that deviates from the plain and simple truth.

Take note of times when instead of saying, "I did it," you say, "I did it because..." or instead of saying "I didn't get it done," you say, "I would have gotten it done if it hadn't been for..." Other excuses include:

- ❦ I'm too tired.
- ❦ I've been so busy and I have so many other things I have to get done.
- ❦ It's too far.
- ❦ There are too many things on my plate.
- ❦ I can't because I am overwhelmed by my circumstances.
- ❦ I did it because I was tempted by another.
- ❦ I was provoked.
- ❦ I never went for my dream because I didn't know how.

> ❧ I said those things because I was angry as a result of something somebody else did to me.

Consider how these excuses make you feel. They might assist you with "dodging a bullet" or placating a situation for a moment or appearing to come out looking better instead of worse, and yet, the long-term, festering effect of the internal aftermath is never worth the temporary "relief" or deferral.

Even when you think you have masterfully achieved avoiding or glossing over something through excuses, if you were not in a state of complete truth with yourself, you know it and that fracture of Self-Separation continues to live inside you. It will come out in all kinds of interesting ways as your life unfolds.

Instead of following this path of excuses, we invite you to consider living in the powerful ownership of yourself and your choices through practicing truth with no hiding to whatever degree you find it possible or enriching to do.

❧ ❧ ❧

Living Your Life Without Defenses/ Defensiveness

Imagine for a moment peacefully and openly living your days without that old, familiar feeling of a need to be on guard or defend yourself against the actual or perceived attacks about the way you think, choose, and live. Really, right now, take in a few deep, slow, releasing breaths, allowing your shoulders to truly relax, softening the restrictions in your body and mind and open to the knowing of your—perhaps currently camouflaged—Self-Connection, Wisdom, and innately known Well-Being. There you go...and breathe....and breathe...and continue.

"Your guard at the door"—your ready state of defense—can travel with you for a variety of reasons and yet, the basis is usually one of two things. Either you are not living in complete truth with yourself about the motivations for your choices, so you are quick to Shield or Hide when you are asked a question about them, or you are reacting to actual or perceived Judgment.

Therefore, if you wish to be free of this restrictive and stagnating practice, you will need to become completely honest with yourself in every moment. Be clear with yourself about why you choose the way you do, including if you do it for the purpose of manipulation of yourself, or someone or something outside you.

No Hiding. You really can't fool yourself. You always know what you are truly up to. So, when you attempt to be dishonest with yourself in any way, you cause a confusion in your system that, in turn, causes an internal separation.

Your aspect of Defense will be happy to oblige you by causing an eclipse of your Self-Connection, making it possible for you to deny the truth and guard you against any internal or external challenges to that moment of dishonesty. Yet, somewhere in there, you know the truth and it hurts you to feel the Betrayal of Trust, causing a fracture in your relationship with yourself.

This is similar to a situation that would cause a fracture in a relationship you have with a friend. If you see that friend do something, know what the truth is, and yet when you ask the friend about it, he or she denies it happened and refuses to acknowledge your truth about it, a fracture occurs. Though you may choose to continue the friendship despite this behavior, your ability to fully trust the friend to be Honest and Trustworthy is diminished, if not completely severed.

Having this kind of mistrusting relationship with yourself can have far-reaching effects that impact your ability to truly Embrace, Love, and Believe in the self. The lure to hide, sidestep, and bend the truth with yourself and others is indeed powerful and may bring you temporary relief when dealing with choices you wish you would not have made. Realize that the emancipation of releasing your defending practices and telling yourself and others (when necessary) the truth instead, will bring you and your life permanent change. It is well worth the Courage and Admitting required to live in a true state of Freedom and brilliant Self-Possession.

This choice to be fully Honest with yourself will also offer your relief from your fear of Judgment. Once you are in a state of Truth and honoring Self-Possession, you will discontinue harshly judging the self. And when others question or judge you, you will know who you are and what is truth inside of you, which will allow you to know that you are always well, even in the midst of others judging or challenging you. You will remain Sure and Confident in your choices. That is feeling sure not from a sense of righteousness or cover, but rather from a knowing that you think what you think and do what you do because it is a matter of who you truly are in your complete awareness of you. Then, when someone asks you a question or perhaps questions you about something you are doing or choosing, your response can simply be, "It fits for me," without Forcing or Judgment—your own or your fear of the other person's.

Now, that is not to say that you will never choose to consider changing something about how you think or who you are as a result of interactions with others. You may very well invite opportunities to mix it up a bit and shift spaces of yourself internally to welcome more Love, Playfulness, Awareness, Connection, Expansion, and so on, into your life. We always encourage you to reinvent and open pathways within the self to allow for such things. The trick is to do it because it is a Match to you to do so, and not because somebody else thinks you "should."

Remember, always be your own biggest influence. No more Shrinking to hold your ground. No more holding your breath. No more using your energy to Protect or Dodge or Concur. The result of releasing your defensive reactions is just the simple freedom of purely knowing and embracing the self in all of your moments.

Living Your Life Without Blaming

Where in your life are you falling into the unfulfilling trap of Blaming? This is a key way humans give themselves away. The moment you say or infer through belief or vibration that something outside of you is responsible for your undesired circumstances or experiences or choices, you give yourself away. No exceptions.

We agree that your world is full of circumstances, and you are the person who gets to decide how you show up for them and what you take away and into your current and future experience from them. That is the truth.

      ❦   Finances—a result of your choices.

      ❦   Love life—a result of your choices.

      ❦   Friendships—a result of your choices.

      ❦   Success—a result of your choices.

If you don't believe you are the one who got you into a situation, then you can't believe you are the one who can get yourself out of or beyond it, either. We can hear some of you reading this and screaming to use your big, loud "BUT..." in reference to this teaching. Scream away. It remains true.

Once you understand and absorb the truth of this teaching, you will know that you are unstoppable by anything outside of you in reaching your desired creations and manifestations. Your life is up to you, not anybody else.

Without this knowing, your stories will continue in the line of, "I tried to be successful, but the economy crashed, so now I am in debt and don't feel secure about my future." We say, "OK." Meanwhile, the person next to you is using his or her Cleverness, Creativity, Ingenuity, Passion for Change, or Belief in Opportunity, to create continued or even new Success under the same set of outside circumstances of the economy. And we say, "OK" to that as well.

You tell the story; we activate the Weaving to bring you what you need to make it so. You choose what you use from the Weaving to manifest your outcomes. That being so, you might wish to begin by telling a story that you would like the activation of the Weaving to provide for, don't you think?

Then there are machine-gun-style blamers...

- ❦ It is because of the way I was raised.
- ❦ I had terrible parents.

- ❧ The world is against me.
- ❧ I can't catch a break from society.
- ❧ I came from poverty and I live in poverty. That is just the hand I was dealt.
- ❧ Nobody will give me a chance.

We could go on and we don't feel we need to because there is very little doubt that you have heard or expressed each of these things and many more in your lifetime. Take a moment to honestly consider each of these expressions of Blame. Do they really have anything to offer you? Is continuing the practice of them going to enhance or expand your life?

We fully recognize that the truth is that some of you did experience trauma or struggle in your childhood and some of you still do, even today. And even so, no matter what has come before in your life, when you stop blaming something from the past, even if it occurred just a moment ago, for the quality of your life in this moment, you become free. You become your own person, living in your own skin, choosing your own Self-Identifiers in much more powerful and life-inspiring ways than blaming will ever bring you.

Go ahead, dig inside the treasure of yourself and pull out whatever it is you need to be Open, Allowing, pulsing with your desire, no matter what your outside circumstances are. You have everything you need right there inside you. Use it all! Your life is truly up to you and absolutely a moment-to-moment design made from your choices. If you don't like what you are living, change your design by changing your choices.

When you run into a "challenge," consider not spending your time trying to figure out *why* there is a challenge. Use your energy instead to decide how to show up for it and how to continue to move toward your dream of you and your life, even with the challenge in play. Remember, you can lose yourself and your dreams by blaming things outside of you for your not having them yet. Or you can take a breath, remember that you are Infinite and Unstoppable, and create a life that feels the way you choose for it to.

Telling yourself the truth about your Participation or Non-Participation in all the events and circumstances of your life is also imperative for releasing yourself from the life-stopping trap of Blame. Just like with Defensiveness, Blame will halt all good things from flowing with ease in your life. The only key you need to turn to stop this from happening is the key of truth.

If it is important for you to find your place of peaceful resolution with your understanding of what exactly happened to bring you to a set of challenging circumstances, you can look back over your life. There, discover what Resentments, Anger, and "No Fair" statements you have lived through the energy of that may have provided the fertile ground for the creation of the "challenge." Just be careful not to move into that neighborhood. Complete your brief exploration and move on, remembering that you choose what to carry forward and what to leave behind in the beautiful tapestry of your life history.

Remember, you are a chooser and in that, there is infinite power. You have a full-access pass to your Freedom of choosing all the time. You get to choose what every moment brings to you by how you show up for it. You have everything within you to take you where you choose to go, a complete treasure chest or arsenal (however you want to consider it) of aspects to use in any degree, combination, and frequency you desire. It is your life. Instead of blaming the bad stuff—and sometimes the good stuff, too—on people or situations outside of you, step into it and truly live on your own terms.

In all this consideration of releasing the practice of Blaming from your life, it will be important for you to include in that consideration no longer taking on the blame for things outside of you, either. Please know that we are not talking about not taking responsibility for your part in situations and circumstances around you. You actually have some responsibility for everything you participate in, including being part of humankind. "Participation" is very different than taking on Blame.

Here are a few examples of such invitations to take on that you might be familiar with receiving or offering:

- ❧ Why did you make me do that?
- ❧ Why didn't you stop me from doing that?
- ❧ Your great idea got me in big trouble.
- ❧ It's all your fault that it turned out this way.
- ❧ My life is a mess because of you.
- ❧ It is your fault that I am not happy, abundant, whole...

You get the picture? We have witnessed many of you take on or offer Blaming to such unreasonable lengths of fiction that we marvel at the cleverness it took the wielder to cast the deflection or blame out at another. Yet, so many times, the receiver takes it in hook, line, and sinker. Then you mix it with a little Guilt and a side of Shame for your failure of another and indeed, failure of yourself. What a recipe that is for Devastation. Yowsa!

We invite you to pause for a moment and make a choice to remember that each and every person is the powerful chooser and Creator of his or her own life, including you. From that frame of reference, consider how it might feel differently for you and others to create your lives by making adjustments to how you address these moments. Compare the feeling you get when reading the following statements through Self-Ownership—instead of the Passiveness and Self-Abandonment expressed by the above acts of blaming:

- ❦ The truth is that I chose to do that.
- ❦ The truth is that I didn't stop myself from doing that.
- ❦ The truth is that my going along with your great idea got me in big trouble.
- ❦ The truth is that it was through my own creation, in making every one of my choices, that everything turned out this way.
- ❦ The truth is that my life currently feels like a mess because of all the choices I have made up to this point.
- ❦ The truth is that my Happiness, Abundance, and Wholeness are my responsibility to create and nurture.

When you don't mix these internal recognitions with Self-Judgment, and instead, receive them as the gift of telling yourself the truth—which frees you to make a choice about continuing to practice them in your life or not—it becomes a powerful and life-catalyzing way to live.

Your choice, of course: the Emancipation that Truth offers or the emptiness that Hiding through Blaming brings.

❦ ❦ ❦

Living Your Life Without Justification

This leaves us with Justification, perhaps the most perplexing teaching of the four areas for you to understand. Many have said to us, "But, Mary, I feel as though justifying or explaining my actions or thoughts helps others to gain understanding of why I am who I am and do what I do."

The catch with this line of thinking is that one has to have clear discernment as to whether the person is justifying his or her actions—or himself or herself. We find that often, it is the latter, done with at least some degree of desperation to be believed in. Even when the justifying is done in conjunction with an apology and request for Forgiveness, if the apology is offered in Earnestness and Truth such as, "I am sorry that I was cruel or thoughtless or neglectful..." and the Forgiveness is offered in Earnestness, then no justification is necessary. If a Justification or Explanation is required, then neither the apology nor the forgiveness is whole and real anyway. That is simply the truth. We realize that this may take some getting used to on both sides.

So, while we recognize your desire to offer justification so you can be understood as reasonable, we wonder what is motivating your need for the other to understand. What is it that you are really seeking to achieve or receive through this justification of yourself or your actions? What happens if you explain and the other still does not understand or agree? Is your urge to justify or explain coming from the inside out or the outside in? Are you doing it to satisfy yourself or somebody else?

Know that if another person is challenging you to explain yourself, chances are the other isn't really willing to hear or have the explanation make any difference in how you or the situation is being perceived anyway. In these instances, the only true Justification or Explanation would be that you made a mistake or that you are choosing to practice yourself in a way that may not satisfy them.

You could go off on a tangent about why these things are so and yet, the simple truth is that you did something and you will either choose to change it in the future or you won't. In these instances, if you choose to offer Justification, be sure that you are justifying the *situation* and not *yourself*.

You see, if you are truly just offering insight about yourself to another from a confident, authentic space within you that is not attached to other people's agreeing to or endorsing you, then you are simply sharing yourself with others.

However, so many times as we witness this activity, it comes fraught with agenda. In such instances, the energy of the revealing is about so much more than sharing yourself openly. Varying agendas may have a requirement for others to "see it your way," so you can feel Seen and Understood, or maybe even put you in Control of the situation. It may also be used in association with Blaming or Deflection, which allows you to "get off the hook" for something or to get back into somebody's good graces. Justification may be used to sway an opinion or to render you Worthy because you have a good enough reason to exist, at least temporarily.

We invite you to be at peace with yourself through Self-Truth with who you are and how and why you choose as you do. This will result in your losing the need to justify or explain yourself. You may instead truly invite people to know you. You may share yourself freely and you will have no need to convince or sway others to understand you because you will already understand yourself edgelessly.

Ahhhh! Now you know the way to Inner Peace.

You Exist, You Are Real, and You Cannot Be Proven

What is the nature of your own existence? Perplexing question, isn't it? To even begin to answer this question, you must first know that you actually do exist. That you matter. And, that the whole of creation would not be whole without you in it being you.

There is one among the nine of us—Horatio—who talks of the days of giants, with a beckoning invitation for each and every one of you to open back up to the giant inside of you, so that the energy of your planet can once again hold the vibration that will allow the giants to return. That vibration was lost as humans agreed one by one to become lost to themselves, lost to the infinite and edgeless existence that you once all thrived in within yourselves.

While some of you are responding to the call of awakening your Inner Giant, we find that when we look at the whole of humanity, there are still great numbers who do not only lack awareness of the giant within, they actually do not, in most moments of their lives, truly know that they themselves exist. This is a rather precarious situation, because when the energy of the humans was no longer thriving enough to hold the vibrational space for the giants to live among you, they ceased to exist on your planet.

So what do you suppose might happen if you stop offering the vibration for existence itself to remain on your planet? The good news is that because of those of you who have made a choice to release the spaces of Separation inside you and return to union with yourself, the world, and the Oneness, there is a momentum growing for the reclaiming of your Self-Existence. This is not an existence separate from others and instead, in Union with others. That is why you are seeing so many more uprisings in your world. There is a call-out to take the Self—one's own authentic and rightful existence—back from where it had previously been given away, lost, or allowed to be taken. Reclaiming the Self is the rise to true awakening and ascension into a free and less embattled way of existence.

If you consider for a moment all the things we have discussed in the foregoing pages of this book, including our words on Excuses, Blaming, Defensiveness, and Justification, you will realize that we have been identifying this practiced embattlement with life, the Self, and one another. All these ways of moving with your life, while perhaps confused as a way to claim the Self, have kept you from living and thriving in the Well-Being of your own existence.

We feel and see the Ache to be Loved, Safe, and Seen. To prove that you matter, that you exist. That is so important. We see the deep, deep desire in each of you to simply be cleanly Received by one another, without correction or remolding to make you good enough.

One of the challenges to being Loved, Safe, and Seen is that people have forgotten to be receptors for one another. To acknowledge and appreciate themselves and one another on any kind of consistent basis that does not have some requirement or exception to it. In response to the fractures that occur from this failure to find pure receptors, humans erect "guards at the door" for so many spaces within themselves.

So then, this drive to prove yourself as real through what you do, say, think, and believe, pulses through that Ache and actually takes you away from the True Self, causing even a wider gap of Separation within you.

The "guard at the door" doesn't only keep you separate from others who may not be operating at a level that even begins to know how to receive themselves—let alone you—The "guard at the door" also keeps you separate from yourself.

We would like to let you in on a big "secret." You are REAL and CANNOT BE PROVEN. So is everybody else. That which is REAL can never be proven. Something such as Love, for instance. If we asked you to prove that your love for a person is real, you could not possibly do so. You might point out actions and moments that indicate its evidence, and yet none of these things are proof of the love. They are just ways of demonstrating love. Love is just so or it is not.

Actually, once love is required to be proven, the love that it was before the requirement for proof is gone. The requirement diminishes and dissolves its original form. That is not to say that a new existence of love, perhaps an even more extraordinary one, cannot be birthed in its place. However, what the original love once was will never be again.

You are also real, just as the existence you are, ready to be Received and Celebrated. Once asked to be proven by yourself for self or by another, the you that you were before the requirement, evaporates. You continue to exist and to be powerful and beautiful in your existence, but never the same.

Audience: Mary, what is Ache?

Mary: Are you wanting to know what it is or what it is that causes it?

Audience: What causes it.

Mary: The lack of receptors in your world and the resulting constant need to prove yourself to try to acquire them.

Audience: I am not sure I understand that. What do you mean by "receptor"?

Mary: Well, that will involve a story. Would you be willing to receive it?

Audience: Sure, it if will help me move this Ache I am feeling.

Mary: (*smiling*) We really wouldn't offer it in response to your question if it wouldn't, but we would like to ask you, would you be willing to receive our story just because we are desiring to tell it, even if it did not help you with that Ache?

Audience: Yes, I would love to hear your story.

Mary: We thank you. We would like to clarify though, we didn't ask you if you would be willing to *hear* our story. We asked it you would be willing to *receive* it?

Audience: What is the difference?

Mary: Well, let's explore that, shall we?

Audience: OK, but things are starting to pile up. We need to talk about what causes Ache, you wish to share a story, and now we are going to talk about the difference between me hearing or receiving your story. I just want to make sure that we don't forget to get back to my original inquiry about Ache. I really want to be able to make a shift around that.

Mary: Oh, we assure you that we are already addressing all three. Are you paying attention?

Audience: I think I am.

Mary: OK, then we will continue. How does it feel different to you when somebody *hears* what you are sharing with them and when somebody *receives* you through what you are sharing with them?

Audience: The first one feels kind of flat because all I know is that they were standing there and what I said was heard by them, but I have no idea if it meant anything to them. With the second one, it feels good to think a person would actually receive me through what I am saying. Like it mattered to them and to me that I shared what I said.

It also makes it feel important to me to pay attention to what I am sharing if it is actually being Received. And, feels inviting to share more if there is actually somewhere for it to go where it will be Honored and Enjoyed and maybe expanded on.

Mary: That answers all three things we have begun to address, then, doesn't it?

Audience: Hmmm...

Mary: The cause of much Ache in your world is the lack of being Received accurately or even received at all. That is what the story we wished to share with you was about. Many people have become separate from the Grace they hold inside to be truly available receivers of one another. This not only causes an Ache in individuals; it causes an Ache in social systems and cultures. Because of this grander Ache, individuals have a sense of Separation and perhaps even a Void within themselves and within the world.

So, when we make a simple request in response to your question for you to receive a story we wish to share, your panic button goes off and causes you to make sure it will not take anything away from you or get in the way of you getting what you came for to find your agreement to do so.

This isn't because you are a bad or uncaring person; it is because you have been living such a long time in the energy of Not-Received that you feel as though you are in a constant battle to get your place in things. The general, overall feeling is that there is not enough to go around because if there were, you would have always been Received.

This confused belief, conscious or unconscious, causes you to shut down your receiver to assure you don't lose any ground and... and... and...

Thus, fractures are born and you develop a practice of offering less and gaining less than your authentic, natural being knows you require to live a joy-filled life and, ta-dah, Ache is born and festers inside you until you agree to open to the innate Grace within you and become a Receptor. It is at that place that when we ask if you would be willing to receive a story we would like to share, you would light up with excitement and say, "YES" because you would know that it can only bring you something wonderful to be a receptor for it.

And, when you open your receptor, truly open it, and shift your formerly held energy into open, receiving energy, you will draw to you the people, opportunities, and experiences who have receptor energy in them, too. It is then that you will lose your Ache. Not because you were trying to get rid of it, but because you stopped living yourself in a way that is so foreign to your authentic and natural existence.

Audience: (*Thoughtfully nodding head "Yes"*) I get it. Thank you, Mary.

Mary: Thank you.

Fractures ~A Call for Repair: Come Home to You

A multitude of experiences, such as the one we have just addressed in the previous chapter, can cause what we call a fracture. In considering fractures, it is important for you to really allow yourself to know that nobody—including you—ever has been or ever will be broken. Please take the time to sit with this knowing and breathe it in deeply until you begin to resonate with its truth. All humans are always whole. However, fractures, large and small, are common occurrences in your existence. And when a person is creating through the energy of fractures, the outcome can be countless stymieing internal and external choices, actions, and practices.

Fractures can occur as the result of the actions, inactions, and words of others. You can also cause them yourself , and sometimes wittingly or unwittingly offer the seed for fractures in those around you. In addition, alas, you can also make fractures a part of your internal home of self on a regular basis. Once a fracture registers and is not immediately cared for, it either seeks a place to hide to give you some relief, or it festers and churns, finding many ways to attempt to resolve itself through your actions and choices in how you move with the world.

The interesting thing about these fractures is that when they have been temporarily stuffed away and then reemerge in your experience, they are simply coming forward as a "call for repair." They are actually signaling you that it is important for them to be revealed and chosen around so you may have a clearer path to your dreams and visions of yourself and your life.

Many people get confused and move into the fracture(s) and live there for a great deal of their lives, believing they have no way out and yet, the only reason the fracture showed up in the first place was to be resolved, healed, and lovingly repaired.

If you can relate to this—and we will offer to you that the truth is highly likely that you have been living in the energy of a fracture or series of fractures—we strongly encourage you to consider scheduling a move-out day because that fracture energy is not your home.

The fracture is actually an element or result of an exchange or multiple exchanges you have had with someone(s) or something(s) in the world. It is not an element of the original self. Your home is within you. Your own unique existence is whole, intact, and unprovable. Live in this whole self without edges. Come home to you in every moment. You belong. You are received.

REMEMBER THIS ALWAYS: You are not the result of a series of experiences or occurrences in your life. You are a life who experiences a series of occurrences in the life you are living. You are free.

In Closing... (and Opening)

In the time before I actually finally sat down to write these pages with Mary, it sometimes felt like a completely overwhelming thought to attempt to translate the significance, powerfulness, and joy of their teachings into just a few pages of a book. Gratefully, through some nudging from Don, our publisher, and many others who so desired to have a book to hold and absorb, I endeavored to accomplish a way of writing by actually putting my fingers on the keyboard and calling Mary through.

The book through which you have just adventured is the result of my treasured time with them there. In the end, I am pleased that the chapters of this book offer a beautiful introduction to the edgelessness of Mary's teachings. In this moment, as I sit in joyful wonder of what all there is still to share of Mary, I smile in the knowing that this book has found and will continue to find its way to all of the hearts, minds, and souls who are ready for it. In turn, it has offered and will continue to offer all love, all celebration, and all freedom to each one of you.

We look forward to moving and playing into the edgeless forever and all that is still to come with you.

With edgeless love,
Jacque and Donald Nelson

A Space Behind the Heart
by The Poet of Mary

There is a dream that lives in the space behind the heart
You need to wear special shoes to go there
It is a space unvisited by most
Feared by some
and known by those who choose
to go beyond that which is recognizable

There is a space behind the heart
where the dream lives
You need special wings to go there
It will be important to pack your wisdom
and your courage to say "Yes"

There is a space behind the heart
where the true dream lives
You need open eyes to enter
It is an uncomplicated, vivid and whole space

There is a space,
just behind the heart
where You live
Where you are the dream
There is nothing greater
than the truth of the self
that caresses the heart

You have everything you need to know the self there
To dance the self there
To write the self there
There is no distance between this space
and the Center of God
There is a space behind the heart
Where the dream knows itself to be the Truth
of the Truth,
of the Truth,
of the YOU that is GOD

There is a space beyond the heart
That inspires the mentioning
That whispers the horizon
That transcends all time

A Space Behind the Heart

It is a space of Echo
The echoing of the beating
of the rhythm
of the fullness of the self
and through the vibration of the echo
the wholeness is transported
through its vibration
to return you
to the center of you
the center of God

There are a myriad of stories in your world
that tell tales
inspiring and frightening
whimsical and serious
Loving and wrought with dastardly deeds
and yet, the only true thread of all existence
gleans in its knowing that it is love
which is what is real

And that which all other things stem from
your are the rhythm
the echo and the dance

Living Without Edges

the oceans deepest roars

most congruent rhythm

on the floor of the ocean

move in perfect harmony

with the truth of you

Matched in pitch and volume and voracity

There is a space behind the heart where beauty is born

and it moves through your eyes

and drifts through the particles of all creation

to become manifest as life

You are the center

now, then and

Forever......mmmmm...........

Let your eyes remember,

your heart sing

and your soul wonder into the infinity

in Union

with Truth

You are the dream and the dreamer......

Glossary of Terms

We offer this Glossary because Mary, through their choosing to bring us a language that is more closely aligned with Living in Union, sometimes expresses words and phrases in a way differing from their common usage.

The following descriptions are the result of Jacque sitting with Mary, asking Them what each meant, and then requesting that They be brief in Their explanation.

Agenda: A need to control or manipulate in some way what occurs with something you share outwardly of yourself or your gifts. Practicing through agenda holds you and the recipient hostage instead of allowing multitudes of new possibilities to birth as a result of you freely sharing.

Aspects: All of the ways you show up in yourself and in the world through your emotions, feelings, sensings, practices, and so on, such as Doubt, Joy, Love, Dread, Scarcity, Wonder, and on and on.

Blanket: Consciously or unconsciously covering up or dodging the divine complexity and range of all you are feeling, sensing, or processing by offering one word or expression to describe you in a moment or a series of moments. A way of condensing or denying the self a whole recognition.

Breathing Your Own Breath: Being your own true self in your infinity of possibility without tangle or trespass. Free and sharing yourself and your life as you choose, derived through Love that is of loving with no Requirement, Control, or Containment.

Causing Your Way Forward: Consciously choosing your way into your next moment and next and next through your own true will.

Choice Point: An extraordinary moment when you have given yourself full permission to speak the whole truth about you or a situation to yourself, with no hiding, and are clear to make your movement forward honestly.

Choosing: Your freedom within to design and create and become all that you are in each moment of your life, through whatever course you call forth within you in the moment.

Confusion Point: Life-altering, misinformed belief about yourself based on something that occurred in your life that you responded to by believing that what you had thought to be true must not be accurate.

Glossary of Terms

Defined: Believing you are what others define you to be or what you believe that what you are is the roles you play, the status you have achieved, the things you are involved in, and so on.

Disregard: The chosen action of not caring about or considering the fracturing impact that your choices may have on yourself, another, or any other particle of existence. This is not to say that you need to make your choices based on the possible outcomes. It is to offer that being openly aware and honest with yourself in all moments regarding any possible agenda or ignorance you are choosing, may be more beneficial to your true and flowing happiness than you may know.

Interestingly enough, when originally created, Disregard was an editing aspect with the sole purpose of automatically editing out of your awareness of anything that was not Truth, before those things even had a chance to register with you.

Dishonor: To not recognize the intrinsic and equal Value and gift of Self or another, by intentionally acting as though it has little or no importance.

Ethereal Breath: The element of your breath, your life force, that is associated with the infinite, non-physical Self.

Exchange: The infinity loop of shared existence, excited to offer and receive in every moment, without Fear

or need for Guarding. Also without Agenda or
Requirement.

False Fear: This is created the moment Shame weaves
with or becomes tangled with any of your aspects.
Shame completely changes and severely limits the
relationship you have with yourself and your life.

Fear Neighborhood: A portrayal, image, or feeling of a
neighborhood within you that is made up of houses
that individually and sometimes together hold the
energies of all your False Fears.

Fracture Point: A moment of disconnect within caused
through exchanges, words, actions, or inactions
in your world that left you feeling Confused,
Unreceived, or Vacant.

Free Will in Union: Your own unique way of being,
choosing, living that is exquisitely matched to your
true and free vibration and the gifts you bring to the
world. Yourself expressed outwardly, without need
for Fear or Restriction.

Held Breath: A moment when you disconnect within or
stop the momentum of your preferred continuous
self in response to False Fear of one kind or another.

Holding Space: An internal non-physical "storage room"
where you put things to address later or never address. Usually creates physical or emotional discomfort as your being knows it is not natural for you to

"hold onto" these things, whether you are giving them conscious thought or not.

Living from the Inside Out: Discovering and creating your life in your own personal expression. Choosing and creating through taking things in and discovering what they reflect or inspire—or do not reflect or inspire—in you. Basing yourself, your life, and your choices on your own true Self instead of on what you believe or in fact what others would like you to be or do so you fit in.

Loft View: The clear, unobstructed, and vast view of the whole of all Creation in every moment.

Match: The recognition of what aligns with or feels good to you and moving with that.

Not a Match: The recognition of what does *not* align with or feel good to you and moving on.

Pain Prisons: The emotional knots and traps you lock yourself in when you hold your breath and forget you are well. The spaces of Non-forgiveness, Ache, Regret, or Worry within you, to name a few.

Particles: Vibrations of energy that form and un-form in Union with truth-filled Choosing.

Self-Identify: Knowing and living yourself and what matches you from the inside out.

Reach: Energy that is always active, moving, changing, creating, alive, receiving, shifting, free, and holds no Requirement or Preclusion.

Real: What is so.

Reality: What is illusion, changeable by perspective or perception.

"Real"-ized: To become consciously one with and activate in you what is Real about or of something, for instance, "I have 'real'-ized the love I am in the whole of me."

Repeat Energy: The duplicating of that which has already been created. Does not activate or engage the imagination.

Self-Evaporation: This occurs when you allow yourself to believe that something or someone else is more Vast than you are and therefore, you shrink sometimes to Evaporation in its presence.

Self-Invitation: Truly valuing and recognizing yourself as Important and Desirable enough to bring yourself with you all of the time, into all of your moments. Looking to yourself for Insight, Feedback, Exploration, and so on, in all situations.

Separation: The implied, practiced, or misinformed belief that there is distance between you and anything of the Oneness.

Separation Hypnotism: A powerful, energetic infiltration of implied disconnection within Self and between Self and all that is in creation. A persuasion to remain under a spell that you are not of or do not have full access to the Oneness and therefore are not powerfully connected and of all things always.

Showing Up: Being actually present with you and with whatever or whoever you are exchanging with.

Tangle: The confinements, traps, or complications in relationships or exchanges.

Trespass: An infringing, dishonoring, or disregarding movement coming toward you from another, or from the Self toward the Self, or from the Self toward another.

Truth Neighborhood: A portrayal, image, or feeling of a neighborhood within you that is made up of houses that individually and sometimes together hold the energies of all your Free, Supported, Cared For, Real, Possible Self in expression.

Union: The knowing and practice of being of the Oneness, expressing yourself and ecstatically recognizing all others as equal and divine Value. Sharing with one another freely, without Requirement or Tangle. A constant state of recognizing the gifts in all moments and the more each difference brings opportunity for birthing next.

Weaving: The magical connecting of all of the dots in perfect flow and response to all simultaneous choosing from the Loft View, where all occurrences are seen and known at all times.

Withdrawing Participation: A conscious choice to discontinue an action, way of thinking, pattern, something you are involving yourself with, that is not serving your shifting desire for Self. It is always helpful to begin this process by telling yourself the truth about your current participation.

You Are Real: You are so, you exist, you are a true life.

About the Authors

In March of 2000, Don and Jacque Nelson sat down to meditate together, calling in guidance to answer the question of "What shall we do with our lives?" Little did they know that this action would dramatically and joyfully change their lives forever, resulting in thousands of people through out the world being immeasurable touched and richly deepened by Mary's insights, love, and guidance.

Since then, they have embraced and welcomed the essence of this presence known to all as The Mary Group to become their treasured work and service in the world. Through the purity of authenticity, Jacque gracefully allows the connectivity of Mary to move into and through her, providing a voice to translate this complete love that Mary has to offer the world. This is combined with the grounding presence of Don, who joyfully holds the space to allow this genuine exchange. Together with the Marys, they offer an up-close, personal, and perhaps surprising understanding of our glorious abilities to create and expand our human experience.

To experience The Mary Group is to experience what it is to be truly connected, encouraged with love to live an edgeless existence free of fear, cleared of confusions and tangles. They help us welcome our first breath back from Separation into Union. Every interaction is an exhilarating voyage into the heart, mind, spirit, and soul.

Offerings from the Mary Group

Don and Jacque Nelson are ecstatic to continue bringing Mary and their continuously expanding teachings to the world. If you are interested in further exploring any of the concepts, tools, or teachings you have found here, please follow us and The Mary Group at:

www.themarygroup.com
on Facebook at The Mary Group
or on twitter at @themarygroup

They offer this opportunity through a variety of formats:

- Partial and full-day seminars
- Week-long adventure journeys with Mary
- Teleconferences
- Breathing Your Own Breath Meditation Series
- Uncommon Conversation Circles
- Mastery Circle Studies
- Private Sessions (limited schedule)
- Morning Messages
- Meditation CDs or MP3 downloads
- and more...

To learn more about Mary or to find out how you can find yourself in a personal audience with them, either in a group or privately, or to bring them to your area, please visit www.themarygroup.com.

CPSIA information can be obtained at www.ICGtesting.com
Printed in the USA
LVOW07s0026111213

364723LV00002B/7/P